Things of Substance

New and Selected Poems

For Anna, Martha, Laila and Mishka

Things of Substance
New and Selected Poems

Liz Cashdan

Five Leaves Publications
www.fiveleaves.co.uk

Things of Substance
New and Selected Poems
by Liz Cashdan

Published in 2013 by
Five Leaves Publications,
PO Box 8786, Nottingham NG1 9AW
www.fiveleaves.co.uk

ISBN: 978 1 907869 76 1

Five Leaves acknowledges
financial support from
Arts Council England

Designed and typeset by Five Leaves Publications
Printed in Great Britain by Imprint Digital

Contents

Landscapes

Land of Lost Content

A Guide to Hospitals

Things of Substance

South Africa

Threads from *The Same Country*

From *Laughing All the Way*

Sisters and Others

Landscapes

Mapworks

If you fold Sweden over at Malmö,
Hamerfest will double up with Athens,
the Orkneys touch down in Orleans,
and Reykjavík rubs shoulders with Valencia,
the eastern shore of Iceland covering Minorca.

So there you are, bringing down the Arctic Circle
to less than 40 degrees, a sort of quick-fire
do-it-yourself global warming; or a re-enactment
of Charles XII's military conquests, dragging
his Swedish soldiers south to prise eastern Europe
out of Russia's grip. So far, Europe has resisted
its map-folders, Alexander, Charles, Napoleon, Hitler.

Just now I've done a diagonal origami fold
bringing Baghdad back north of Glasgow.

Night Walk with No Moon

it is possible to have a month without a full moon
we take the kids out as it gets dark   my group
first up the hill behind the house   less light
than we think left in the clouded sky
on the moon there are no high mountains

I keep my hand in my pocket   grip my torch
but don't switch it on   we crunch up the path
everywhere on the moon is sheathed by rocky rubble
the kids hoot like owls   moan like ghosts
while meteoroids and asteroids bombard the moon

the clues on the piece of paper don't make sense
13% of people surveyed believe the moon is made of cheese
we look for a way downhill back to the road
but all we find is a barbed wire fence   we drape
our anoraks over the wire   climb over ourselves

the multi-layered space suits weigh 180 lbs
but only 30lbs on the moon   then the river flashes
in the no-light of the no-moon   we wade through
back at the house the others are already toasting bread
the moon is the only extra-terrestrial body visited by humans

Water Cycle

Yesterday in Leeds I did storytelling with Year 4—
the story of a drop of water, only Mrs Dee said
they had to use connectives of cause and effect.
I nodded wisely and began my story:

Beth was a drop of water in Ahmed and Salim's
rolling-wave sea. Daisy's sunshine evaporated Beth
till Andrew and Mohammed blew ferocious winds
at Hannah's timid cloud, and holding tight to Beth

she hit those very cold mountains, Mariam and Hakim.
Beth cascaded down Sally's waterfall into Jo's plunge
pool and on down the river where Aisha's mouth spat
her back into the still-rolling arms of Ahmed and Salim.

Then I read my poem about Derwent dam and how
they drowned the village in order to make the reservoir.
Aisha's mouth opened wide: "In order to, in order to,"
she sang, "a connective of cause and effect."

Today I see the connectivities of water, a streak of snow
high on Helvellyn, beside me Glenridding Beck falls
over and over into its plunge pools and on down to
Ullswater. East of the watershed the North Sea rolls.

This Is the Corner

This is the corner with the yellow grit-box
hung over with rain-sodden rhododendrons.
This is the stone wall where the ivy creeps
and this is where the rose-bush run wild
has filled the space where the sumach died.

Across the road are the stumps of the sycamores
felled last week to stop their roots lifting the floors
in the house nearby. Here are the neighbours counting
the rings who tire of the job when only half way.
And so on my walk downhill to the park

where a boy drowned in the floods five years ago.
I cross the road with the roaring cars,
the shop-drop juggernauts not helping at all.
And the row of shops that sold bread and fruit
have closed, have closed, just take-aways now.

Lost Time

Years ago, just this time in early March I climbed
from the west, through snow patches on Helvellyn
past the cross for the man who fell, his dog who howled.

Then dared Striding Edge and slid into Patterdale,
leaving the low growl of lead mines in Glenridding.
Now there are only hillside scars and mapmarks to show

where the workings in High Horse and Lucy's Tongue
grumbled all day long; the bothy built into the slope,
its stone arch filled in, iron door bolted, a secret mystery.

Dark green spikes of gorse catch the grey scree falls,
one tiny flower a harbinger of yellow-to-be furziness.
I lean on the wire netting aslant the lichen-spotted wall,

look where the beck slips its stony collars, and bounds
down past larches struggling to come green against
the dark curtain of pines. And my finger tips shiver

because for so many years the one inch map is all
I've had to keep the singing beck in tune, to keep
the dizziness of the mountain spinning in my head.

Happenings

Here I am on Pituah beach waiting
for something to happen, my back
to the towering hotels, the marina.
The January surfers spider the waves
and it's hard to catch them between
breakers that roll them in faster
than the jump of my gaze from
rising swell to broken crest.

The sand is littered with shells striped
brown and pink, honeycomb kerkar,
fused and fossilised dune, grey pebbles
polished wet. If you're lucky you could
happen upon mosaic, bits of pottery,
blue-green glass, red conglomerates.
Today I find a rusted metal disc, a thrown-
away bottle top? Or perhaps an ancient coin

spun from the histories of cliff-top settlements—
Phoenician merchants in Reseph, Greek
Apollonians, Muslims in Arsuf, crusaders,
sunbathers—defaced by the happenings
of centuries. It won't come clean about
its origin but there are two sides to everything
in Israel: a rocket lobbed into a school,
a bulldozer rubbling someone's home.

Incident

We came up slowly to the fort behind the women
red and yellow garments bright in the sun, trees bare.
Was it Ecuador or Goa? I would say it was a fish market
or possibly a baker's stall, flat loaves freshly baked.

We didn't understand the language, Portuguese
or Spanish mangled over centuries of colonial rule.
Our ears were not attuned to these vowel sounds.
The boy in the black and white t-shirt offered

us something. Then we saw, it wasn't fish or loaves,
it was stones from the wall of the fort, where yesterday's
rebels had blown up the building, the dictator still inside.
And as we looked the sun lit up the hole in the wall

and there were things there I would rather not have seen.
But now we cannot deny what we have seen: the doll
with one leg, an army jacket, bloodied, medals torn off.
We turned away from the women, walked down the hill.

Grand Union

And then today rounding the bend in the canal
he saw it again, white walls, symmetrical windows.
And although the hollyhocks had gone, he saw her
there in the garden, back bent, intent on planting—
she who'd always cut what shouldn't have been cut,
who'd always dug up plants when they weren't weeds.

Of course, it wasn't really her. It was a young woman
and how could she still be young after all those years.
But it was her blue blouse, the one he'd bought in Spain.
And her brown curls across her shoulders
and the way she always shook her hair back
without touching it. He put his foot on the chugger
and the narrow boat picked up speed but the Lady Jane
was long and cumbersome and he couldn't stop looking.
The boat bumped and the woman stood up straight
with a slight frown like she'd always had,
waved her trowel with that familiar flick of the wrist.
"You can moor up here if you like." He wanted
to go into reverse but it was twenty years too late.

Winning the Farm

I did not tell my husband
about the farm and the cherry trees;
how I had put my name down in the lottery.
I did not tell him about the fjord, the blue water
and the cherry blossom. I did not tell him
how I signed my name in blue biro
on the dotted line; and for weeks I forgot
about the farm and those terraces of cherry trees,
covered in silver plastic against the white frost.

And I went to the office every day and moved
the cursor over the blue screen; and I wrote
important emails for my boss, and came home
and cooked an evening meal for my husband—
cooked carrots and turnips and never thought
of the farms where carrots and turnips grow
in brown earth before they are washed
and packed in plastic bags.

And at Easter my husband said: "This summer
we will go to New York." But the next day,
a blue envelope fell on the brown mat: it was
from the Gunnar Bergsrud estate and I had won
the farm on the edge of the blue fjord
with its white cherry blossom.

So now we shall not go to New York
but to Kipstrand to the Bergsrud farm
with the white cherry trees spread with plastic
all along the blue fjord and there will be
red cherries for all of us.

Landscape Painting: Finland in Snow

The snow is deep, cold. The swirl of wind
has swept it up against the tree trunks.
The surface glistens with a blue shine.
I stand in the window, September
sunshine warming my back.
Beyond the glass, geraniums and hydrangea
are pink, red and yellowy cream.

But I'm not looking out of the window,
I'm looking into Finland, a forest landscape
somewhere between Helsinki and Hanko.
There's not a breath of wind, no movement.
I'm waiting, someone must come soon.
Otherwise, what am I waiting for?
What will they want me to do?

Combs

I have started a new collection—
four-star hotels, and their bathroom
baskets, shampoo, conditioner, gel and spray.
And best of all, the combs.
The Sunny Capital in Beijing offers
white combs in sanitised white paper.
Shanghai's New Asia has them packeted
in mock red damask, and proper handles.
The Tang Cheng in Xian has pictures
of the terracotta warriors.

                        They must have been
adept hairdressers, these warriors.
Perhaps they each took a step forward,
worked on dressing the head in front of them.
Or perhaps they did their own, as skilled
with comb as with sword or bow and arrow.
The officer would shout: "Attention—hair!"
and out would come seven hundred thousand
combs, to sweep the owner's long black hair
into a topknot tied with coloured braid,
a left side topknot to leave space for
the right-handed flourish of sword;
right-side topknots for the kneeling archers—
freedom for the left-handed stretch of bows.

After battle, they'd let their hair down, comb
it out. Now these warriors have lain two
thousand years, heads and arms knocked off,
topknots still intact, uncombed.

The Great Wall

Suddenly skyscrapers give way to a chain of hills
and we see the wall snaking away in the distance
so we're in the film ourselves now. Polluted mist
turns the evergreens to evergreys. At Badaling
the bus climbs to the Juyong Pass and the Emperor
Qin's tourist stop. The Ming dynasty gate-towers
give easy access. I'm grabbed by the north wind,

buffeted by the street-vendors: "Hello t-shirt,
hello scarf, hello lolex watch, all very cheap."
Like a well-trained tourist I pull down my hat,
shake off the vendors, shout "No, no, bu yao."
I'm ready to walk two of the five thousand plus
kilometres of wall in the face of vendors and wind.
"Turn right, it's difficult, turn left it's very difficult."

Through the first watch tower and on to the wall,
reconstructed and iron-railed for extra pull-up,
room for ten abreast, or five horses, the roll of
mountains framed by the crenellations. Under
my feet the stone-shine of centuries hides
the cries of Emperor Qin's buried-alive labourers.
According to Chinese wisdom I am now a hero.

Tiananmen Square

Kites are flying like pigeons:
whole flocks on strings swoop
to the ground, then rise again.
At the far end, Chairman Mao
keeps watch from his portrait.
No-one knows if it's his body
in the tomb where he's flanked
by stone revolutionaries forever
stepping into a future that's gone.

Beyond the Forbidden City, new
buildings scraping the new skies,
have left behind Hu Wan Li and
his family who mob the tourists,
knowing there is no food at home,
no fire to warm the cold of March
and tomorrow nowhere to live
when the bulldozers roll in to
flatten their little Hudong houses.

Someone takes my photo with Mao
behind me. I keep my eye on the kites.

Rolling Rain and Happy Fish: Shanghai

Through rain into the old city with Starbucks,
Macdonalds cut into the upturned eaves. I watch
goldfish swim on each others' backs, jostling

like the tourists on the marble bridge above them,
then find *Peace and Comfort* in the *Yuyuan Gardens*
by the *Pavilion of the Rolling Rain Curtain* to

the *Clear Stream down the Hills Pavilion*, and
the *Pavilion for Enjoying Happy Fish*. A semi-
circular bridge is hidden by overhanging trees—

pink almond blossom floats on the people upside
down in the water, strolling among the shoals.
Through Yin and Yang double passages I glimpse

magnolia and ginkgo, plum, orchid, bamboo.
Another corner, and the wall dragon drags
his back along the top, body grey stone tiles,

lobster antennae, lion teeth, eagle claws.
His saliva dribbles into the squat toad's mouth.
Together they will brew storms, but today

there is only gentle rain, and in the distance
a circular arch frames two umbrellas
balanced by the falling drip of willows.

Containers

Most stuff is packed in China, the containers
winched on board, not a stevedore in sight,
someone at a screen and keyboard in control.

I've seen the ships queuing in the sea roads
of the Indian Ocean, seen the coloured boxes
piled up in Durban harbour, some emptied

to become township homes, schools, clinics.
But sometimes there's another story when
Aeolus unleashes the winds from his cave

and the ship, half a mile of it, is no more
than a toy, its little boxes tipping off the decks.
Today the Napoli beached off the Devon coast:

look how easily the boxes spill off their piles,
slip into the water and empty themselves.
Like old-time wrecks, the cargo is up for grabs,

the January sands alive with beachcombers
hauling motor bikes, nappies, coffee makers,
the coastguards helpless while distant folk

drive down for the biggest carboot sale—
everything free to be rolled away in barrels.
And just here and there a container holding

someone's life, pictures, crockery, cushions
packed in Sweden bound for South Africa,
jetsam to be picked up cheap off the sand.

Land of Lost Content

Craven Arms Museum

This is a place of higgle and piggle, the past
captured behind glass and wire netting
falling over itself in its look-here-look-nowness.
Like a zoo where you are more prisoner
than the animals, here you are caught and held
by the dust-dazzle of old things—

things which are spread out, piled up, left
to speak for themselves in moveless appeal.
Only the crackling soundtrack of old songs
keeps with you from decade to decade, from
kitchen to shop, from school to seaside holiday.
Every now and then tiny echoes from your own life,
the ration book, the wind-up gramophone,
the Dundee cake tin, dried egg powder,
will strike through the muddle, throw their weight
about, destroy your own level-headedness,
roller-coast you into the next display, leave
your heart and stomach in the wrong place.

The Gloves are Off

There was a time I wore gloves—

woollen mitts to snow-race down toboggan slopes,
scooping up and rolling the wet stickiness to build
snowmen, to chuck and duck in snowball fights,
blowing breath-warmth through the wet wool;
knitted finger-stalls for my chilblained fingers
cushioned between wooden chair and tunic-bottom
coping with over-heated classrooms, itchy lessons.

Later I wore leather-palmed, buttonhole-stitched for driving;
black, see-through, catch-your-nails for theatre visits,
white crochet for summer outings with my mother,
elbow length, hard-to-pull-on for my wedding.

Now I sometimes resort to wash-the-car rubber
or a cotton-leather mix for pulling weeds,
waterproof nylon for rain-sodden hill walks.

But mostly my iron fists go undisguised.

Clothes Pegs

used to be wooden, knife-sliced by travellers
selling at the door. You just pushed the pegs
their toothless bite gripping sheets, thick towels.
You could paint faces on their rounded tops, make dolls
or get two-year-olds to stick them on a saucepan rim.

Years later came the metal springs on wood:
like mouse traps they'd snap back on your fingers,
jump off the sheeted line, disappear in the shrubs,
hide forever till they'd be too dirty to use.
Now we're on to sprung plastic, rainbow-bright

as toys but springs liable to rust. Today we found
the old wooden sort in a craft shop, painted blue,
red, green and yellow like sticks of rock from
seaside holidays; gave them to Laila, rattling
in the aluminium saucepan my mother used for jam.

She gurgled, picked them out one by one, twisted
her hands till she'd rimmed all ten of them.
Then rain on the window sent us running to get
the washing off the line. Laila, on the kitchen floor,
looked up, sucking a red peg in a bright blue mouth.

Imperial Good Companion

One of those dark, still hot evenings in Israel,
jacaranda petals patterned thick on the grass.
"I've got these old letters," you say, "in a tin box."
We fetch them from the cupboard. Forgotten bits
of paper, thin blue airmail, thick white letterheads.
My handwriting very English, Mother's continental.

Mostly our father's letters are typed, black print
seeping into the paper across the more than fifty years.
So there he is, sitting in the kitchen in the Hampstead
house, the Morrison still in place under the table.
His regrets are there in the purple clematis outside
the window, your post-war UN job lost to the Kibbutz,
red tomatoes grown in a dry Palestine, no Israel yet.

He faces the keys, round, metal-rimmed, ready to thump
his messages of love and warning, a shrill ring at the end
of every line as he flicks the return handle. He knows
you won't come back, your return is with the illegal
people huddling on board ship in Haifa harbour; with
the hanged terrorists swinging in the pit below Acre jail.
The letter creeps up above the roller, curls gently over
the paper rest. He releases the grip, pulls the letter,
a wave of his hand across the keys, across the miles,
signs in flat, elongated script: *Your Daddy*.

"You know," I say, "I've got the typewriter, my first efforts,
the poem about him being such a tease; my story about him
and Mother being secret rebels back in Russia.
And it still works but you can't get the ribbons any more."

The Ice Box

Just a brown wooden cupboard—
intents and purposes hidden inside.
The top-lifting door with its metal clasp
opens right up if you push hard enough
and there's the slithery ice-block drip-
dripping into its zinc container.
You let me help lift it out into a bucket,
the last ice-block ever emptied into
the scullery sink. No more ice-man
knocking at the back door, your curses
when he misses us out, when all the milk
goes sour and the green taffeta sheen
on the joint assaults with its gone-off stench.

We push the ice box aside, its little feet
scratching the kitchen lino. Later that day
the shiny white fridge arrives and we make
ice cream with raspberries from the garden.

Piano

She said I looked like the sort who might play.
Otherwise she'd take out the innards,
use it as a store for potatoes.

Rosewood inlaid with a flower and leaf design,
candle holders of blackened brass, white notes
slightly yellowed, a musty smell of firelit

family evenings singing *Abide with Me*.
She said £10 to me, it was only an upright:
ten pounds of potatoes dropping like semibreves

into the stringless cavity, the black and white notes
silent, the frustrated hammers with nothing to hit,
and the pedals wobbling loose like old men's feet.

I said ok, £10. Now it plays the age-related game,
like the oven door tied with string, the melting
fridge, it's a semitone out and won't pull up.

Bakelite Telephone

It hung on the wall in the garden passage
The mouthpiece mounted on a wood block
opened ready for all to kiss-talk their way,
the earpiece on its brass hook alongside
for them to lift, hold tight, receive the words
threaded through cables undersea and overland.

Grandmother's death came with the robin
who bobbed in from the garden and then
the French voice from Paris earpierced
its way to say: "Elle est morte, ce matin."
Mother came running, grabbed the phone
but she couldn't change the words.

Later when I was still in London, this horn
of black bakelite brought your words from
Belfast: "Strange place this, see you soon."
And in the mouthpiece I recited my worst lies
to your father how I'd been to the *mikveh*,
made myself pure for our wedding.

From Barts it relayed my father's death,
sealed the selling of the family house,
sent you and me to Ulster to a new black
bakelite, square and squat with joined
ear and mouth pieces, balanced nicely
on the crossbar of the telephone frog.

Mangle

Daytime the blue stairs are safe
a landing window all blurred glass
and then the tank room that hisses
and plays ball-cock day and night.

At the far end the washroom, a sink,
a bath and the mangle sitting upright,
a headless bird perched on two legs,
carved iron feet, one wing folded,

the other stuck out like a handle
that turns the wheel of its heart.
Trudie who came from *Europe*
in the middle takes the clothes,

feeds them into the bird's rollers.
A groan and a screech and the bird
pippies a yellow stream of soapy
water into the waiting bucket.

Heraus, says Trudie, her raw hand
in my face, *you bin go late for school.*
For a moment the bird noises stop.
I run, jump the blue stairs two at a time.

Gas Mask

"Tell me about when you were hibernated,"
said Martha, meaning WW2, not hedgehogs.
Today I'm the grandmother-poet come to take
them through it all, history, technology, art
and literacy. With 2D gasmask boxes,
iron rations packed, teddies hugged close,
labels pinned to lapels, voices hoarse with
*We're going to hang out our washing on the
Siegfried Line*, they're ready to be evacuated.

Children wave goodbye to tearful mums,
board the row-of-chairs train, and steam-
chuff their way into the countryside,
while the city mums leap-frog the tables,
morph into farmers' wives, marshal
evacuees to their war-time billets.
The boys do Home Guard whistles,
stirrup pumps, mooing cows, tractors, pigs.

It's as well they don't know what I know:
the rubbery smell as you thrust your chin
into the mask, the clammy breathlessness,
the shiver down the spine, the air-raid siren
wail, the shelter-rush, the high-pitch hum
of planes, *Theirs*, *not ours*; the unlit dark
reverberating with bombs and anti-aircraft
fire in the long wait for the All Clear.

Carpets

She arrives from Iran, hauls
her heavy suitcase to the attic.
I watch her unpack, kneel to lift
out the rolled-up kelim.
I almost thank her for the gift,
but she lays it down,
the kelim is for her, for prayers,
to remind her of home, she says,
her father, brothers and the carpet factory.
For a moment the skylight sun catches
the bright diamonds of Tabriz.

Downstairs to the Shiraz in my sitting-room,
an ancient gift-in-lieu to my father
for the raw wool he sold in Tehran.
I think of the generations of family feet
in the old dining room rubbing a worn circle,
the blue and red twists laid bare to the warp,
the pattern hardly discernible.
I take my felt tips, kneel down, colour out
the years' wear and tears, gravy spills,
dropped crumbs and arguments.

Kodak Brownie

Tiny two-and-a-half by three-and-a half
black and white snapshots—my dad bent
at the knees as if to fit on the photo,
a wicked pixie grin on his face; my toy dog
Tufty Dusty on the front garden wall,
standing obedient, not a twitch or a bark at
the magnolia petals floating above his head.

The Brownie's a hand-me-down, black cover
ungluing itself off the wooden frame but inside
it's all dark magic. I watch my dad fix the spool
in its slot, press the winder in, turn it on to
number one. I don't know about focus, timing,
aperture, the way the shutter blinks like an eye,
how the little brownie takes the snapshot.

I don't know either this spring sunshine day
that somewhere in the United States, another
brownie, George Eastman, who coined Kodak
loving the upright letter K, now shuffles bent
in pain from spinal disease, writes a note to say:
"My friends, my work is done, why wait?"
And takes his own life with a gunshot.

Clockwork

I've not had a wind-up watch for years
yet last night as I unbuckled the strap, finger
and thumb of my right hand went to the winder,
a clumsy slip on the silver fluted knob
the tiny hidden battery forgotten,
remembered only the rasp of skin,
the half-heard ratchetting of wheel and cog
the catch of breath against an overwind,
a fingernail pull that might whiz the hands.

Today at the piano, years since I've played
Solfeggietto, Carl Philip Emmanuel Bach,
my unthinking fingers clock up arpeggios
hand over hand across notes I cannot name.
Then the octave-stretches hammering
a change of key take me by surprise.
Unnerved by treble twist and flutter,
breathless, I let my mind play truant,
leave my fingers to their own devices.

Mincer

Remember how I used to make the breadcrumbs,
the stale bread dried out in the oven, a Friday ritual,
getting ready for our Saturday lunch visitors.
It was the same machine for bread and meat.
The putting it together trick was hard for little fingers,
getting the disc of holes at the right angle, fixing
the container rim, and it needed stronger hands than mine
to screw the whole thing down on the table top.

What I loved was the crunch of crumbs spinning out
of the holes, but even more skin-shivering was how
the pink lumps of dead animal turned into red squiggles
of live meat as I turned and turned on the mincing handle.

You told me to finish with bread crumbs to make sure
all the meat was through. Then I'd watch you hand-mix
the mince with chopped onion and egg into a great roly-
poly you called *klops*, smacking it this way and that
on a board till it held together. You'd smother-cover it
in breadcrumbs ready for the oven. You won't know now
that I don't eat meat, that all my mince is packeted soya.

House Clearance

I walk past the second-hand furniture shops,
wonder who sat on that chair, stretched out
on that settee watching black and white films
on this TV. And that bed, the mattress upended,
the brass bed ends leant against each other
in uneasy proximity, no longer steadying
the sleepless couple who tossed and turned
unable to sleep for whatever impossible reasons.
Their stories fill my head.
I look for the house they might have lived in
where weeds sprout through paving stones,
the paint chipped off the doors. I ring doorbells, knock,
listen for the hollow echo, try a key in a rusted lock,
stare through murky panes, dried hydrangeas on tables.

I take a turn round my own house,
how everything looks ready for clearance,
the worn-out fabric on the velvet settee,
curtains hanging off the rail at one end,
piles of books shoved sideways
like sleepers in a railway carriage,
every surface dust-thickened like skin on milk,
all waiting for the moment, when someone after me
will carry them out to a van parked in the street.
For now my own head filled with projects
I shall never carry out.

A Guide to Hospitals

Operating Table

They turned the playroom into a hospital.
For real, this time. No playing doctors.
That same table where I'd done homework,
drawn pictures, written stories, draped
blankets to make a theatre; run fingers
along the ridged cracks daring the splinters.
Did I climb on to the table myself, throat
tight against inflamed tonsils, anaesthetic?
Mask over face till lions and tigers crawled
all over me. Coming round into playland,
ice cream the only possible slithering food.

Now we are having our evening meal, table
ridges hoovered clean of crumbs, polished:
wild animal placemats, wine glasses winking.
Invited guest a child psychiatrist, we draw
unbelieving breath, as we discover it was
his father did my tonsillectomy on this table;
chloroform thirty years away floating through
the wine bouquet, fills my nose and throat.
The joint is carved, slices of roast beef ooze
blood on to our plates. I laugh, promise
melt-in-your-mouth raspberry ice for dessert.

University of Moscow Medical School 1986

Welcome to Moscow, our great city, our prestigious
     university
here in medical centre we can show you wonders of Soviet
Medicine, everything good for citizens, good for world.
Come this way, this is specimens room, forward, please.

We have pickled brains of important heroes, all in jars.
These brains have done many inventions, many theories,
mathematical, astronomical, psychological, many more.
And over here we have small pieces of human body

but people very famous, have done big steps in our country,
and in universe, in space-travel. Please consider little jar
          here,
man very great in science of space. Comrades, this little piece
of human anatomy, this Gagarin's appendix.

Tel Hashomer: Israel

Watchman's Hill and here I am in A and E
watching, waiting for a diagnosis for my sister.
I run after her trolley as the orderly whisks her
away down dream corridors. A bend en route,
and she's gone, swallowed into a room labelled
in Hebrew. I mouth the letters hoping for a word:
all trah sond, could be no entry. I try again—
alltrasond—ultrasound. Got it. The door is shut.
I wait on an iron bench designed for discomfort.
Nurses, doctors, visitors stream past, their mobile
trails of Russian hover in the air, then fade,
more like Moscow than Tel Aviv.

How shall I know which is her trolley emerging,
no colour, no number plate. I peer at several
strange faces. At last she's wheeled out again,
and, desperate to cheer her up, I sing nursery
rhymes in Russian, Hebrew and English. Back in
A and E, they say pneumonia, she's being admitted.
She's pushed into a forgotten parking bay:
my pigeon Hebrew gets nothing from the receptionist.
Up on the ward a Russian nurse hands me pills.
"Water? where's the water? *my'im, voda*?" I stumble
out of my depth. He points to a sign: "*Rak personnel*"—
staff only. *A'hot*. I'm sister and nurse—the same word.

Stockport Hospital

Done my stint in Israel with a sister not much into walking,
my knee allowing no more than a hobble along the beach
below Apollonia. Always a need to get my feet wet,
North, Irish, Channel, Atlantic, Pacific, Indian Ocean.
So I'd braved the slope and got the Mediterranean over
my ankles, waves splashing my legs on to rolled-up
jeans, no towel to dry off, damp sand clinging to skin.

I'm coming back by plane to Manchester, feet thinking
limestone, gritstone, peak mud, cow-pat fields, stone stiles,
I've shouldered my travel bag, ready to go, right foot poised
above the top step of the movable stairs—splat! the knee
chooses its moment, gives way and gives pain, pain on step
after step across the tarmac and into the terminal till
I hear my own voice call out: "I need a wheelchair."

Ambulance ride to Stockport Hospital and an A and E
waiting room full of Saturday accidents and football
crowds roaring from the overhead TV. After three hours,
an x-ray and a prod or two, the doctor says torn cartilage,
try crutches, then exercises to strengthen thigh muscles:
leg up, ten times, count to six, three times a day for the rest
of your life. Walking in the Peak? As and when.

The Northern General

New Year's day, cold but no rain forecast till later,
so we get out on to Froggatt Edge, sun dodging
cloud on the other side, trees dripping melted frost
and the streams escaping ice, pour into the valley.

I turn to look at Higger Tor, Carl Wark, Win Hill,
catch my foot in a rut, stretch my left arm to steady
my fall. The rut bank comes up, punches me under
the elbow, I sit breathless, think I'll be all right till

pain takes a grip before I can, and I'm not all right.
Clouds get the better of the sun and I'm left sitting,
my doctor sister as helpless as I am. No mobile,
till another walker phones mountain rescue, offers

hot tea and a thermal wrap. Others walk by, smile,
tell me to trust God who will bring help. Thankyou.
My response is to sing till the rescue team bring pain-
killers, and jolt me back to the road and A and E.

Dislocated shoulder, but they can't yank it back
without anaesthetic. When I'm round, we go home
some of the mud off our boots lost to the hospital,
pins and needles in my thumb—damaged nerve.

Two days later, a phone call from the consultant.
How kind of him to care. No, something more
sinister. The crack in the bone's too wide to heal,
please come back. The shoulder needs to be pinned.

Pinned? I've got a thousand pins jabbing in my thumb.
But I go back to a three day stay, hard pillows, dry
sandwiches; green bonnets and masked faces clowning
in and out of consciousness; a lost patient climbing

into my bed; another promising more help from God,
and how lucky my birthday's the 15th of November,
the very day of her Uncle George's wedding—a sign
I'll get better. The pin and pins are with me still.

St Mary's Maternity, Manchester

Unlike exams where you can walk out
when it gets too bad, here I'll have to
stick it out till the baby emerges.

Nobody tells you what it's like.
Late evening October, trees turning
and I'm singing the pain, singing

the unbearableness of it over and over.
The ward is dark, just night lights,
and they leave me alone to rustling

bed-clothes and deep breathing.
I have to keep singing, a sort of
Celtic keening, Gregorian chant

half Arvo Part, half Taverner,
though they're not yet on my music
scene, Part probably not yet born,

still just an unfertilised egg waiting
for sperm so the music can get going.
Crescendo up a chromatic scale till

a nurse comes clopping, bends low, tells me
to shut up, think of the other women here,
they can't sleep for the noise I'm making.

Noise? it's oratorio. Doesn't she know
I sing contralto in the Cantata Choir?
Morphine shuts me up until next day

I'm working hard on the labour ward,
doing a series of syncopated grunts
against the non-rhythm of the pushes

and the heart beat escape of gas and air.
There's no grand finale, only another series
of scenes, hospital-directed: *baby will suck,*

won't suck; lie baby tummy down; on her back;
contraception? can't tell you, I'm Catholic.
The real birth is getting out of the hospital.

Athlone House: Stroke Patient

I don't understand stroke or this wheelchair.
I don't remember today. What I remember
is the cold in Russia, how we lived in Finland,
the crossing to England, The Hall prep school
and my pink and black striped blazer; running
after the fire engine, and Mother getting upset.

My sister, Celie, is here but she looks so old.
"Where is Mother?" I ask. And she says,
"Mother died thirty years ago." I weep. It's
Maria from the Philippines, not Mother, who
hoist-hauls me out of bed, says, "Don't be sad."
"Sad, schmad," I say but she doesn't understand.

I'm fed up with this cruise, the service is poor
and the travellers are so stupid, but Celie
says the women over by the bar are nurses.
Who needs such much nurses on a cruise?
Could be actors, don't want to miss the play:
hope there are enough seats for the press.

Celie wheels me to the green room, weird
rehearsal going on in here. Lot of noise.
This won't get a good review, if I'm writing it.
Celie says it's the patients having tea. I tell her
I have no patience with her silly explanations.
We laugh—she likes my jokes. I like the cakes.

Hampstead General: Children's

A push too far, the garden swing
higher than safe but big brother says
not to worry, he knows how.

On the next swing up she contorts,
takes the curve with her body
but when she's back down

there's a bit of her left behind,
and her stomach pokes out.
There are cries, tears and doctors.

The world hisses with other words,
hospital, surgeon, anaesthetic, incision,
promises of a bicycle if she's good.

Goody, the carer, takes control
beds side by side. There are stories,
but she dreads the chloroform, the pain,

horrors tamed by their conspiracy to
tune in to the palm court orchestra,
switch to Brahms when her mother visits,

but what if the doctor tells on them,
something to worry about more than
cramp or scar-tissue slow to heal.

Xerogeotherapy

Like Monsieur Jourdain who discovered
he'd been speaking prose all his life
I know now I've been on dry land
or so they told me at Physiotherapy,

though you could have fooled me today
as I splashed through rain puddles
holding my umbrella sideways against
storm force winds with my good arm,

the other hanging loose and useless
at my side. The rain lashed horizontal
soaking my coat-skirts and trousers,
dampening everything, cutting visibility

to one yard between my feet and the edge
of my blackbat bedraggled, bent shaft
umbrella. The puddles were filled with
broken buildings, fractured branches

and the cars swept great sprays of water
out of the gutters across the pavements
all over anyone foolish enough to wait
for a bus too near the edge of the kerb.

Once into Physio, they pummelled and
kneaded, hoisted my loose arm on a pulley,
told me it was time now for hydrotherapy,
I wasn't getting far enough on dry land.

Language of Impotence

The move from renal to gynae means all women now.
No more men carrying plastic bags like shopping,
no more harassed male nurses wriggling like fish.
You lose the bawdy camaraderie, gain solidarity:
patients, surgeon, house physicians, all female.

For a week you'll be holed up in a safe place.
Or so you think till the professor comes round.
His firm follow dutifully, registrar, house doctors,
a couple of students. They form themselves into
a curtain round your bed and the professor begins:

"Doctor, would you tell the students about this
lady's condition." Now's your chance, you think.
"Excuse me, not lady, I'm a woman," you tell him.
He stutters in broad Scots, first an apology, then
a defence, turns on the house doctor, demolishes

her when she muddles her Latin endings inside
you. The Cockney woman in the next bed says:
"Shame on yer, don't yer like being a lie-dy?"
Later you quiz the house doctor but she shrugs:
"We're used to him, no point complaining."

The students, one from Malta, one from Greece
ask in broken English what is the difference
between a lady and a woman. Later still when
it's time to take the stitches out, your surgeon
indicates the two doctors: "The girls'll do it."

Chemistry

Formulae and equations, sister and daughter
she listened and tested them both, understood nothing
and when her son started on dark deeds in the cellar
she listened for the underground sounds, hiss
and crack and the sudden spout of flame and gas.
Thwarted, he tired of the chemistry set, looked
for explosions in things political instead, like
John Dee, perhaps, stirring chemical magic
in Prague Castle to frighten the Emperor.

And she thought of that chemist shop in Priory Road
with its jeroboams of blue and green liquid swelling
the windows and how she looked up at Mr Price
above the convex glass counter filled with
forbidden packets of pills; and behind the man,
walls of brown wooden drawers, each with its
brass handle and a hieroglyph stranger than
any Egyptian document studied in school.
And on the shelves, rows of fluted bottles

full of medicine to do you good or poison you;
Famel Syrup for when your chest seized up
and your breathing wheezed inside your tubes;
the yellow liquid burned your throat, the taste
on your tongue could creosote a wooden fence.
Syrup of Figs to cleanse your inside out. Once
her sister disappeared into the dark behind the shop
where Mr Price kept his ultra-violet lamp.
Nowadays she keeps away from chemists if she can.

At the Sangoma Ceremony

Zena's done well in television, made programmes;
now we're watching her, TV camera up against
the wall of this Soweto front yard. Children
join in the responses to the chants: sheissbon—

> *Blessed art Thou, oh Lord our God, King of the Universe,*
> *whose strength and power fill all the world.*

sheissbon, sheissbon: thanks be to our ancestors.
Zena's dancing. Her red skirt whirls above
the clink and rattle of her bottle-top anklets.
Her tutor's drumming, singing, explaining.
Zena's ancestors are Xhosa and Irish:
with imprecations and help from the living
her Xhosa ancestors lead her to the hidden goats,
tethered under an acacia in the neighbour's garden.

> *The kids which father bought for two farthings.*

The goats tug on their ropes but are held till
Zena bends over the corrugated iron sheet, slits
their throats, drinks. The cameras fizz-click
on her blood-stained mouth, ready for breakfast-
TV next week when they've done with Christmas.

> *Blessed art Thou, oh Lord our God, King of the Universe,*
> *whose word makes all things on earth.*

"Sins forgiven," the tutor explains, "now that
she's a sangoma, her name's Nonkululeku,
freedom. She will practise herbal medicine,
help the sick." Thunder over Johannesburg
brings rain: storms build slowly in Gauteng.

We hurry inside for tea and sandwiches but first
we place a coin before the kneeling Nonkululeku.
She sprinkles it with spices, mumbles her thanks.

Blessed art Thou, oh Lord our God, King of the Universe,
who makes sweet-smelling wood and plants.

Zena-Nonkululeku waves off the cameras, promises
her consultation fees will be reasonable. We drive
out of Soweto not quite sure of the route back.

(The blessings in italics are taken from Jewish prayers)

Transpennine Train Operating Company

I like to relax on train journeys but this girl is making me
        nervous
I'm reading *The Immortal Life of Henrietta Lacks*, stress
        enough.
        A photo of Henrietta with her hair in a 1950s quiff,
        her neat suit

but I keep an eye on the girl opposite me: she plugs in her
        hair straightener,
don't know if it's ionic, ceramic, tourmaline, rapid heat or
        infrared,
hope it won't stop the train, aren't the sockets meant for
        laptops?

        Henrietta doesn't tell anyone there's been so much
        blood, that she's going to Johns Hopkins. Dr Grey's
        not seen a cervical tumour like this before. But he
        harvests the cancer cells—I'm drawing short breaths

as the girl takes her brown wavy hair, handful after handful,
        runs them between
the hot bars. We're in the Totley tunnel now so she's there in
        the mirrored dark
with her bag of make-up things, colours and creams spread
        over the table.

        Dr Grey starts treatment, sews in the radium tubes
        and Henrietta lies there wondering how the family's
        doing without her, especially baby Joseph. They send
        her home with a bag of antibiotics and constant
        pain—deep breaths—

The girl applies her cream base, then rouges her cheeks, for
        work, her boyfriend
or maybe she's going to audition for a circus clown. Lips
        next, bright pink.
Eyelids shadowed blue, and then a black brush to the lashes
        like shoe polish.

*On her next visit, Dr Grey takes more cells, doesn't
tell Henrietta. She dies but her cancer cells keep
growing, they're not ordinary cells, cancer cells. She's
buried in a lost grave and her children don't know
about her immortality.*

Now I'm really worried, because this girl's things are still all
        over the table
and we're past Stockport. Look, we'll be at Piccadilly in a
        moment, I shout
at her in my head which is still marvelling and weeping over
        Henrietta.

*The Lacks family don't know how every lab across
the world has HeLa cells which grow and grow, only
know there's no work for them in Turners Station or
Lackstown. Nobody thinks to tell them. Sixty years
till this book gets written.*

The girl has managed to get all her belongings back into her
        bag just in time to
get out at Piccadilly. I go on reading beyond the airport,
        across Europe into Asia.

Things of Substance

Hands

In their time these hands have gone through a lot—
itched with chilblains, thrummed with pins and needles

gripped the dentist's chair-arms, then relaxed
into the creeping freeze of gum and lip

sifted sand drifts on the beach
torpedoed through breaking seas

played the piano stretched beyond octaves
memorising the shape of sounds

reached for hidden blackberries, got scratched
morphed into spiders, praying parsons, comforters

kneaded dough, plasticine, unknotted muscles
grabbed a child back from a cliff, a kerb, a swimming pool

they've waved to the wrong people, been sat on, shaken
done their bit of wanking, washing, wringing out

they've been held up, caught red, been one over the other
and under
when all they wanted was to be asked for, lent and given

Stars and Moon

Once I remember we were lying in the grass, August,
and above us just stars, city lights blotted out beyond
the Welsh hills. Didn't really know one from another,
hill or star. You said, "Look, Pleiades, shooting stars."

Then an owl hooted and its wings brushed the pine tree
or was it the wind. And you echoed the hooting till
you and the owl roped in every star and every hill.
I lay very still, said nothing. Silence. No moon.

Last night late I looked through the window hoping
to catch the supernova they'd been talking about,
east of the saucepan handle, they said to look,
but the mottled clouds were giving nothing away.

Then suddenly, the sycamore tree opened its net of leaves,
and there was the moon, escaped from cloud, stuck tightly
in the branches, and somewhere up Sterndale Road
an owl hooted and I forgot the supernova, thought of you.

Sculpture

Don't is the word that goes with touch.
But today I am allowed to close my eyes,
lose sight of the printed warnings, and
hands washed, dried, talc'd, I find

the bronze head ready for my blessing.
The curly hair first to the finger tips,
then greedily palms over the face till
one finger traces eyebrow, eyelid

and me not knowing if these eyes
are looking down the snub nose
to the gentle hardness of open lips.
Then both hands again round the neck

over the abalone ridge of each ear till
I translate what I have felt into what
I have not seen, know that in my touching
the sculptor has touched me.

Skin

(For Esther)

To think my skin is the biggest part of me
bigger than the curlicues of my brain,
than the labyrinth of my intestine, my heart—

my heart—huge enough to take
the poundings, beatings of the missiles
that hurtle every minute of every day.

And yet, with the wringing of hands comes
the palliative touch of your own skin on
your own skin—rubbing away what hurts.

When I visited you for the last time I tripped
on your crazy paving, cut a three inch gash
in the taut skin on my knee till blood poured

through the hanging flap. Staunched with a scarf,
I phoned for help. At the hospital, seven stitches,
the flap sewn down in and out through my skin.

I didn't tell you because your own skin was
stretched tight on your legs, red and burning
with ulcers that wouldn't heal. My scarred

knee took weeks for the skin to grow together.
Yours never did. Sometimes when the purple scar
on my knee fizzes I think of your crazy paving.

Cold

slipped in to the house as I left this morning
has been in possession all day, skittering
from floor to floor, sliding the radiators;

knows I have trudged home through snow,
hat pulled over ears against wind and sleet,
hands curled tight inside worn-out gloves;

ignores my shudders and shivers when I come in,
dares me to take off my coat and hang it up,
sneers as I click buttons, fill hot water bottles,

laughs at my numb fingers that won't obey
when I bend to undo the laces on my boots,
positively giggles when my sweater rides up

leaving a rim of unprotected flesh. I think of bed
where I might escape but what if cold is lying in
wait on the icy sheet, under the too-thin duvet?

Hear Hear

He says I have to wear this hearing-aid
for ever and ever. Amen.
You'll be able to hear the mice in the wainscot,
he says, the flare of gas as you switch on the grill,
the drip, wait for it, the next drip of the kitchen tap,
the sigh of the laptop as it turns itself off.
All right, I say, it'll be a new world,
I can listen out for—

the angels brushing their wings on the roof,
the murmur of conspiratorial devils in the cellar,
the inward suck of bees dusting the polyanthus,
mercury shooting up the thermometer on a July day,
and the clatter of one star against another as they jostle
the night sky for ever and ever. Amen.

Conjugation

We did all the verbs anyone could think of—
paralleled the Latin *amo, amavi, amabo*
with *I love, I have loved, I shall love.*
Then *amor, amatus sum, amabor*
with *I am loved, I was loved, I shall be loved.*
Strangest was *I might have been being loved.*
I think it was the future imperfect, conditional passive,
in the grid in the bottom right hand corner of the page
and it made no sense when I was twelve.

I would have to wait, put up with years of *I love,*
first Gilberte who was in my class, had blonde curly hair,
and was half Belgian but she was more interested in Jill.
Then the boy I passed on the way home from school:
he was tall, and had a smile I couldn't quite be sure of
but it was mostly for the girls in the hockey team.

I mouthed the tenses past, present and future,
tried passive and active voices quite shamelessly
with Arthur who had invited me to the May Ball;
jumped moods from indicative to imperative
with Eddie in the B and B at Stratford-upon-Avon.
After a bit I gave up, made do with conditional
and imperfect boy-friends who stood me up, let me down,
with partners who put me down, slagged me off
till I found myself more dependent on prepositions—
in and out of, with and without, and finally against.

Singing

I've lived with you for so long, sometimes
I don't even notice you're there. You buzz inside
my head like a bee caught against the window pane,

audible, but untouchable; and I have to coax you out.
Sly thing, I'll say, you've got as far as my larynx,
you're on the tip of my tongue, and then you slide

back. Your shyness is all pretence. All right,
I know my lung capacity doesn't suit you any more,
my diaphragm won't budge for you, and my brain

turns your words and tunes inside out, back to front.
But you know and I know, we depend on each other,
I need your snatches of Bach, wisps of Schubert,

bits of Russian nursery rhyme, French cabaret.
So why tease me with the persistent possibility
of your prima donna non-appearance?

Hurdling

I've always wanted to hurdle
but I've never quite managed it.
I dream of that fly-over feeling,

what Hopkins called the "achieve of it".
I would like to be able to get over things
but there are some things I can't get over

like the people who hesitate, then move
to another table although there's
plenty of room where I am sitting;

or other people who go away
when you thought they were staying;
like people who are ill and might die;

or the fact that sometimes a poem is
grounded and even when it goes the full
hundred metres and the right leg does fine

with an ecstatic lift, there's always the follow-
through leg that won't perform and brings
the whole thing down at the last hurdle.

Boxer Shorts

I'm a regular Palooka when it comes to hanging out
boxer shorts. They won't hang up evenly—
always scrunched and the waistband too thick
so the pegs jump, fly somewhere out of sight
in a flower bed where you won't find them
till next year when they are all dirty with bits of mud

stuck in the spring, the pegs, I mean,
but the boxer shorts meanwhile are boxing
clever and you can't get the top over the line
to fix the next peg, and they're really fighting
dirty now, below the belt, but even if you manage
a clinch, they don't dry properly, the waistband

is so doubled over the line, it's still damp
and then you bring the boxer shorts inside,
or rather you try to, but they're too short to stay
over your arm, and too piled up to stay in a pile,
so they scatter like a walkout bout, and you're
grovelling on the canvas, punch drunk, ready

to throw in the towel, only that's still on the line.
In the end you're saved by the bell, someone
at the door, so you just do a southpaw, dump
the whole lot, you're down and out, but
there's no-one at the door when you get there,
and you've had enough already with boxer shorts.

Double Voice

You're always there wobbling on two uneven legs,
looking at me out of one eye, the other screwed shut,
one corner of your mouth up—*c'mon smile*,
the other down—*enjoy being miserable then*,
like Lancelot Gobbo and his conscience,
when I'm just trying to be easy come, easy go.

Today as I leave the house, the snow lying thick,
you say, *walking boots*, and I say ok,
but when I've got them on, struggled with the laces
you turn around and say, *what's wrong with shoes?*

It was like that when Tom left. You said, *accept it,
it's ok, you're better off without him.*
So I planned a holiday in the Isle of Man
but when I got to the docks in Liverpool,
saw the Liver building, the birds and boats
on the Mersey, you said: *Fancy, this is his town.*

Boats

They're indecisive wobblers, two-faced, coming and going,
and there's no being certain even when they're tied up
in the harbour. You can't trust the knots, the ropes.

They're always shuffling, wanting out, wanting away,
haunting with rigging-tinkle music. And their silly names,
The Daffodil, The Red Rose, The Mary Ann, The Lily

as if there was to be a May Day dance, when really
their sly names are a cover-up for rust, engine oil
crates of smelly fish, and drowned fishermen.

I think of that first-ever sailing trip on the Danube
and the blue is a complete lie, it's dark and murky.
I couldn't tell which way to lean, and the wind

just took the sail, laid it flat on the surface of the water
and I in my summer skirt lay flat alongside the sail.
I swam ashore, dried off, went for *Kaffee mit Schlagsahne*.

Next trip on the Solent, crew to an old school friend
who was less of a know-it-all sailor than I thought.
I did my best to duck under the swinging jib, hang out

whichever side she shouted, marvel at the water flow.
Then the wind dropped so we did things to the sail,
switched on the motor, but the boat was obstinate,

in league with the wrong sort of tide it seemed.
When the motor failed, I made the boat move
by gripping the gunwale and it got us back, just.

How the Grass Grows

I love grasses for the linearity of their leaves
for their colours even when withered,
the wine-red of Japanese blood-grass,
the white gathering of gardener's garters.
Over there by the hedge, the dark-leaved
drift of red-hook sedge, the plumes of pampas
and the fodder-bound blue of field fescue.

I have collected seeds from their flower heads,
watched for water stress, impoverished the soil
with gravel and pea grit. Now I must dig up
and split the clumps, avoid the vicious teeth
on leaf edges. I must pull ivy out by hand,
groom the grasses for dead leaves, wait through
the withering of winter for next year's growth.

Bells

Oranges and lemons ring the bells
and then comes the chopper for your head.
So I know bells can come to no good—

they bring and ring no good—
they belong to something strange, a church and I do not
          belong.

At night the clappers billow-boom and I cannot run like the
          clappers.
My ear is pressed into the pillow, and still they come for me.

My mother brings me a cow bell from Switzerland
which makes no sound, and later I will hear them gladly
with every shaken head on the mountain pass.

But the child cannot muffle their harbinger ring,
tolling and telling the Germans have invaded.

It is years later I steal into Durham Cathedral and the rope
hangs loose in the crossing—pull me, ring me, the great bell
tolls and I am the ringer, the bringer of telling.

Sand

silica and other particles ground and beaten by the sea:
the world slips through my fingers grain by grain.

Port Stewart, honeymoon sand dunes, climbing till breath's out
beyond fear of a strolling sandfall that would fill your mouth.

And the dunes again at Sandwood Bay, held by marram grass,
honeymoon over, the recurring body slip and push for foothold.

Today at Crosby, past the Georgian villas on Marine Parade,
I cut across the sward, climb through these bring-back dunes

to the beach where the wind blows it up into in my face,
a horizontal hurricane, dry sand streaming over the wet.

Signs warn of gullies, quicksand, fast incoming tides; tell you to
keep within 50 metres of the path; oh I'll beware the blow-by-

blow grains of sand, but a hundred rusting figures, pinned ankle-
deep in sand, ignore the coastguards' warnings, defy the sea,

and backs to the dunes, silhouetted in setting sun, look towards
a place where their empty heads imagine other possible worlds.

Chalk

Born in London's chalk basin I know about hard water
the soap that won't lather, have skip-jumped
the smudge of pavement art on Hampstead Heath.

And the nail-tingle screech of blackboard chalk,
dug from the Chiltern scarp-face, school set
in the white chalk-face of Bucks' flat vowels.

And the white vapour-stream of a German plane
writing its challenge in the summer sky, sends
us scrambling into the chalk-walled shelter.

Oh the May blossom blackthorns lining hedges
and the tractor turning brown topsoil, ploughed-
up chalk hilled from Bledlow Ridge to Hughenden.

And I've tasted the furred-kettle on my tongue
at the drained teacup's rim. And the flint-cum-
chalk downs along the south coast, Beachy Head,

I've jumped that cliff down to the deckle edge
sea in all my holiday dreams with the horror
of rice-pudding not eaten in the boarding house.

Calcium carbonate ninety million years of making
in the coccolithophore seabeds. Now I chew it
every day, Adcal for my disintegrating bones.

Carbon

It's manufactured me and I manufacture its lethal
compounds: together we leave breathed-out, exhaust-
ed footprints. Its diamond allotrope's a must-have:

my grandmother's brooch, de Beers and Cartier,
blood of the miners in a Victorian setting, sore
fingers of the women cutters, cleaving the rough,

bruting the girdle, blocking pavilion facets,
setting the table facet into the dop, polishing
for the Rajahs, the countesses to buy and flash.

The graphite allotrope, its hexagonal layers of atoms
a powdered lubricant, or a conductor of electricity.
And sheep-marker Grey Knotts graphite for writing

so soft the end snaps off in the pencil-sharpener and
you begin all over again: shavings a-flutter, the point
wobbling in the wood, nothing like a diamond.

And coal, that carboniferous under-the-earth old-tree
allotrope; how I crawled the coalface at Creswell
Colliery, helmeted, gloved and knee-padded, jumped

the coal-belt as eyes sparked in dark-faced miners
roaring the cutter, how their washed skin blue-veined
their temples and dust coughed in their lungs.

I've sold the diamond brooch, and the carbon bonanza's
on its way—buying and selling emissions. *Make a killing
in the new carbon trading market: roll up, roll up.*

Salt

We've been warned off it but couldn't do without it.
We've sat below and above, shaken it and thrown it
over our shoulders. We've done the briquetage

for over eight thousand years, evaporating sea water;
sentenced prisoners to years of salt mine tunnels;
sprinkled it on wine-stains, slippery doorsteps, roads.

Looked back to Gomorrah and seen Lot's wife turned
into a pillar. Heard (to be taken with a pinch of salt)
about Roman soldiers getting their salt-based salaries.

We've walked up Salter Lane, down Salt Box Road,
been to Salzburg though more for Mozart than salt.
Marvelled at Benvenuto Cellini's gold salt-cellar with

Neptune and Ceres lounging round the bowl. Salted down
layers of herring in barrelled vats. Eaten our salad greens.
Brushed our teeth, rubbed it in someone else's wounds.

Loved the shiny blue packets in Smith's Crisps. Learnt
about ionization of sodium and chlorine, passed the NaCl.
We're the salt of the earth and we know we're worth it.

Intrigued

by paper, the blankness of the blank page,
the scrunch of crunching it into a ball,
its stiff resistance and its half-spring back
into a shape that has no meaning.

by paper folded into crane and flower,
no way of remembering where to begin and end
with valley and mountain folds, pleats,
reverse folds, squash folds, and sinks.

by Mrs Delaney's cut-outs, meticulous
tissue paper flowers botanically accurate,
one thousand of them cut and glued on
to a black background, her paper "mosaicks."

by other people's backs-of, the letters
from insurance, police, department stores;
notes they've taken, essays they've written;
subscriptions to magazines, organisations.

by Britney Gallivan's record for paper-
folding: 12 times and MIT claim 13, 000 feet
of toilet paper with uni-directional folds
will fold thirteen times. I'm happy with seven.

by the Mobius strip twirled round its own axis,
cut down the middle so a crawling ant could
go round and round for ever on the same track
never reaching a boundary, never reaching...

by Escher's prints where his frogs and leaves
jump and morph one into the other eternally
tricking our eyes, stairs rising to nowhere
only to come down again and again rise.

Knowing the Names of Wild Flowers and Birds

Yes, yes, I can tell herb robert from campion
pink petals starring grass and hedgerow high and low,
and bluegloss taller, darker than speedwell.
But with lady's smock and shepherd's purse, I'm not sure
if his eye's on her ankle or she's after his money.
And then vincula, valerian, one of them hides a blue face
in low-lying green, the other stalks through wall and fence
without so much as by your leave.
                                        And for years I thought
simkins were sparrows, their twitter flown in from Sheffield
streets to Longshaw lakeside. I know black and white magpies,
the song of blackbirds on the aerial announcing evening,
but if I'm watching that swirl high up on the thermals
above the heather, how can I tell if it's buzzard or kestrel.

You knew them all and I was impatient when you stopped
to name them as we walked the coast on that holiday
in Brittany. As you got older the birdsong cut out but if
I could pick the flowers now, I'd press them, dry them,
send them by post but then you're not there to receive them.

Angel

I only saw his wings for the first time today;
they opened out just as he came to the door.
From my bedroom window I looked down,
saw him bend to put the two white pints
on the step—and there on his back, half-
folded against each other, two white wings,
his blue overall cut out neatly round each one.

I wanted to rush downstairs to greet him,
but afraid he might fly away like yesterday's
ladybird, I knocked on the pane. He looked up,
smiled beatifically, flew back to his milk van,
the empty milk crate slung underneath him
like the basket of a hot-air balloon.

Walking on Telephone Wires

I've been practising in the garden,
tied my son's skipping rope to the holly bush,
fixed the other end to the shed door handle.
Today I'm ready for the washing line.
The white plastic shines in the sun.

First I walk a parabola shadow on the ground,
wonder how I shall get up there.
The aluminium steps are light-weight—
I place them in the brambles on the wall.
I'm off, head up, looking forward to
tomorrow, the high wire walk
along with the magpies and starlings
when I'll hear the reverberating telephone
talk through the soles of my feet.

Hedera Helix

The new leaves, innocent pale, cling
like baby climbers to the stone wall,
crawl over the edge. Time to weed.
The little ones come away to my fingers,
then with cajoling and tugging, long
threads unravel a greenleaf jumper
that unstitches itself in my hands.

How one thing leads to another,
blind alleys becoming sighted.
I wind the ivy into resistant balls
that spring undone on the rubbish tip
ready to re-knit. Raised veins on
the backs of my hands and the twinge
in my wrist, residue of ivy-pulling.

Holding On

While I write this, a mosquito zings in a boy's ear.
While I think of the next line, a tin of coke has been
sprung open and drunk by another boy.
He has never met the first boy—his skin is a different colour.
A girl in a nearby street sings a lullaby but does not sleep
while another girl in another street endures the cut
and stitch that make her marriageable. Somewhere
a man scratches an itch, a woman tries not to scratch.
There's always a place where a mango is ripe, falls
off the tree and no-one notices. An insect crawls
into the orange flesh and still no-one is there to see.
Always a child laughs and claps hands for no reason
and always a child cries and the mother cannot fathom
the reason for the cry. Somewhere a guitar twangs,
somewhere a guitar string snaps—
While I read through what I have written, a fire in a place
I've never heard of consumes someone else's words.
There is only one place where all these come together
and like a kite in a wild wind, they are being wrenched
out of my control to fill their own moments without me.

Inventing the Slipper

The slipper doesn't take even steps,
it's almost as if like a fish the slipper
slides with a body flick that takes her
ahead of herself, ahead of everyone else.

Most at home on ice or polished floors
but can swish on wet surfaces and of course
good with the odd coin, can slip it into
or out of your pocket when no-one's looking.

Likes the waterfall of silk and nylon down skin,
the throat-stroke of lemon smoothies, gin and tonic.
Abhors rubber gloves, tight jeans, high boots.
Coughs and splutters on dry roasted nuts.

Sometimes goes her wicked way, oil-slicking
the sea, sliding between the wing feathers
of birds till they become one slippery ball
and all their jagged flight has been oiled away.

Sometimes gets between cup and lip, spoils
the best-laid plans, but then allows us to slip
out the door unseen, and when we're back home
after a high-heeled day, there's a real welcome.

The First Avocado

That was the first time we'd eaten an avocado
the first time I'd cut through that animal skin
pulled it apart and stared at the stuck-in stone.

I jiggered the stone out and laid each half
in a little dish, stunned by the pale green flesh,
dripped vinaigrette into its welcome bowl.

We spooned up the first mouthful, together
in time, let the oil and vinegar run to the back
of our tongues, melted the stuff in our teeth.

We looked at each other across the table
in that tiny lean-to kitchen in Belfast
and I, the Scorpio, had scraped the skin

clean in a few seconds, while you, the Virgo,
relished each slow mouthful, precisely.
I watched you, impatient for the next course.

That first stone planted in an earthenware pot
has grown tall, its green leaves drooping on to
my window sill. But there's no avocado.

Wool Gathering

Look high in the hedge, blackthorn clouds
blow white against blue of sky and sea.
Here, low-down mists of wool caught
on the brambles streak the long arms
of the dark-red dead blackberry stalks.
The wool clumps festoon and hang
like the froth of cuckoo spit; are blown
in the whitened wind. Flashes of sunlight
turn single threads into starbursts.

Imagine the huddled sheep struggling
for a hedge place to rub away loose wool,
wanting rid of their thick fleeces. Or maybe
they come to the field-edge to nibble
the longer grass-shoots of new April growth.

Now back on the sunless side of the house
the soft wiriness of the gathered wool
lies inert, its white shine reduced to a
yellowish grey on the table—pulled wool
is deceptive. Think washing, carding,
spinning, dyeing, all before you can
cast on, knit your woollen sweater.

Wool Scales

Like fish or roof shingles, hidden under the microscope,
the cuticle of each fibre not at all the way I imagined it
over the years—smooth and comforting, but scaly.

Not so much the cause of scratch and itch, but danger
in washing: the shrinking, matting, irreversible once all
those scales slide invisibly one on top of the other, on top of...

I never realised how much I needed its crimp: the helical
curvature of each fibre, the uni-planar wave of the staple; how
I should have known the micron measurement of each diameter.

I knew wool was hygroscopic, absorbed and released moisture,
that it kept you dry and warm. And now with scales scraped,
hydrolysis by protease, I can machine-wash my woollens.

The Names for Wool

The burr-catcher, skin-scratcher,
bloom dipping, dag-stripping,
the grease-holder, fleece-folder.

The shorn fleece, the grade-increase,
the wrap-around, the pence-per-pound.

Scour and card, teasel-hard.
Comb-sort, tops-long, noil-short.
The spun thread for worsted,
hand-loom deft for warp and weft.
Tenter, fulling, felt and dye
fibres fine please the eye.

The sell-by-ounce, the won't bounce.
The pullover, wool-over.

The skein-winder, ball-binder,
the dropped stitch, the hairy itch.

The tease the cat, the pull-on hat,
the gather-garner, sock-darner.

The loopy one, the droopy one,
the stretch and shrink, the fibre-kink.

Body-warmer, wind-stormer.
Sweater, jumper, shoulder-humper.
The hold-the-heat, the sweat-the-feet.

Keep-out-rain, reduce-the-pain.
Blanket-maker, cold-taker.

Cushion-cover, carpet-lover,
scarf, hat and hand-glover.
Cosy tea, embroidery.

The Wool Mark, the Wool Sack,
the Wool Exchange, the Wool Pack.

Merino, Shetland, Romney, Swale,
Cheviot, Clun Valley, Wensleydale.
You've named the sheep where they're found:
wool's your staple, safe and sound.

(With apologies to Anon and Seamus Heaney: The Names of the
Hare*)*

My Father's Hats

There he is in the Czarist Army—an officer's hard peak cap
just for parades. Paid his way out before the fighting started.

At his sister's wedding in Helsingfors with his new wife—
a black silk topper, so silly on such a short man.

No photographs of his own wedding, secretly in Brussels,
        maybe
just bare-headed in the registry office, my mum already
        pregnant.

A business trip aboard ship to the USA, before air travel,
a trilby pulled down low like he might be going to join the
        mafia.

A black bowler for work in his 1930s City of London office,
suspicious-looking as the thief in *Emil and the Detectives*.

The red fez with a black tassel he brought back from Morocco
made us all laugh. And he'd sat cross-legged to eat kebabs.

Once he took the Siberian railway to Uzbekistan, came home
with feel-good wool, and an embroidered skull cap.

There's one of him on Brighton beach, just before he died,
squinting into the sun under a sailor's cap. Who's the girl?

At his funeral we couldn't help sniggering at my brother
holding on to our father's Anthony Eden in the graveside
        wind.

South Africa

(some of these poems appeared in The Same Country, *Five Leaves, 2006 and some in* Dancing with Delsie, *Leaf, 2009)*

District Six Band in Derbyshire

Isolated in backwater rural Derbyshire,
not far from British Rail, now Bombardier
Transport where South African Gautrain
has just begun to snort through its sexy nose,
those farm and quarry kids I taught twenty
years ago had hardly seen a black face.
Today, as train engineers they're meeting
the Gauteng fitters, talking assembly points
and World Cup Soccer ready for 2010.

Back in the 80s the London District Six Band
brought by jazz-mad Dermot workshopped
music with Year 10s: the drums went
sounding through the school, echoed
the quarry blasts of the white limestone
worked by their dads; the saxes deafening
the garment factory's midday hooter,
the lambs' hillside bleat drowned in
the beat of trainers on wooden floor.

Last year in Cape Town driving through
the still derelict District Six under Devil's Peak
I imagined the Friday smell of pickled fish,
the weekend greetings of holiday cousins,
re-heard the rainbow shouts of kids off school,
the bands playing, drum and saxophone, then
remembered how Dermot and I, Irish Catholic
and Jew, told the Band we understood dismember-
ment, diaspora. *No you don't, you're not black.*

Arriving

Flying in early morning and how do I know
where I am after eleven hours of drumming
through the dark. I watch the flight details,
losing height but we don't come right down:
we hover at five thousand feet, it seems,
until I realise this is where I'm at,
Johannesburg is that far up.
The passengers are white but at the airport
everyone's black or almost black. Outside,
it's still cool for December, but Father
Christmas gets used to the heat here,
and as the car speeds down the highway
we could be anywhere modern and hot
until we leave the new development,

and there's African art and craft, carved,
woven, beaded, laid out along the pavements,
and the houses have barbed wire all along
the fences and gates, so high you can't see over
because this is a rich suburb. Soon,
we're in Houghton and Yeoville with black
and white people thronging the market stalls,

the coffee shops, the supermarkets, and I'm
somewhere different from anywhere else
I've been, not Stockholm or Helsinki,
or Paris or London, or even New York.
If there's anywhere it brings back, it's
Israel, because of the heat, the landscape,
and a jigsaw of people that won't quite fit.

Swimming to the Wreck

You walk to the edge, a thirty-something clown
in yellow flippers, waving your snorkel. I sit
on the hot sand below the Robberg, the fat

Dutch name for seal mountain. The white villas
of Plettenburg Bay sprawl into the green of
the fynbos for miles along this coast.

Now you and Mark dive into the breakers, swim
away from the shore until you are floating heads
under the rainbow halo of the midday sun.

Somewhere in Cornwall thirty-something
years ago on cool sand beside an elephant
rock, two boys pump up their dinghy, paddle

out of the cove, disappear into a sparkle of
sunlight. The coastguard's helicopter circles.
Hours later, they row back, unaware.

Today's adventure is different. I jump up
to identify the curved backs of dolphins
swimming towards you. They circle the dark

patch which marks the wreck where you have
disappeared. I sit on the sand doing nothing,
my mental contortions unable to pull you out.

Then two heads surface, gradually grow arms,
and I'm will-powering every stroke, till
the breakers body-surf you on to the beach.

You describe the shoals of fish threading colours
through worn timbers, beautiful and dead scary,
worth every minute of your struggle and mine.

Comparatively Speaking

He never seemed to get a kick out of
saying one thing might be like another.
"Let each thing be what it is," he said.
That first hot summer when we watched

cricket in The Parks, for him that was all
there was to it, but for me the long gap
between each click of the bat echoed
the impatience of a child waiting for

a turn at croquet on a Hampstead lawn.
Here at Nature's Valley the Indian ocean
rolls on to the sand, I am desperate to take
the waves, break them on the Côte Sauvage

in Brittany, stumble through the dunes, not to
this lagoon but to the quiet Baie de Quiberon
though if he were here he would only say
that what I've got now has to be good enough.

Cape Town

First view is from Sir Lowry's Pass:
high above Somerset West and Cape Flats,
the townships of Khayelitsha and Mitchells
Plain just shimmer in the hazy sun.

So we drive down from the Hottentots-
Hollands, mountains that pour their clouds
over the side like woollen waterfalls
and the highway takes us to the back of

Table Mountain. They've hidden Khayelitsha's
shacks behind a fence: if you drive fast enough
you get a running glimpse like old flicker books
that make movies out of still life.

Now we skirt the hillside and come out into
Table Bay and there's the town, its skyscrapers
dwarfed by Table Mountain, the Twelve Apostles
and further on the Lion's Head and Signal Hill,

hardly bigger than the early settlement when
the Dutch and British came in from the sea,
first saw the white cloud layer spread across
the Table, with blue sky above and beyond.

We're staying in Camps Bay through Kloof Nek
overlooked by Apostle number three or four.
The house, newly built, seems like Monte Carlo
1930s, flat roof, white, picture windows to

the sea. Inside, it's all black leather,
plate glass and ironwork, uncomfortable.
The landlord, Greek-Canadian, nouveau-
riche, seems to accept that Apartheid's

gone, well sort of gone: Maria comes
from Khayelitsha by taxi, every day, to wash,
iron and clean. She's Xhosa but her language
is lost in her deafness. Her little sister helps

out over the holidays but the silence around
us is thick. They are hungry for the coffee
and cake I offer as if breakfast was not
a meal they'd known. They smile thanks.

On Christmas Day we sunbathe in the garden
above a blue sea where the Benguela current
ices the South Atlantic. The Indian Ocean
rolls in warm but the currents don't mix.

Why This Night Is Not Different

"Why is this night different from all other nights?"
The youngest son turns towards his father.

Tonight I'm marking Passover in a strange
house with new faces round an extended table.
The family are remembering not only the Exodus

from Egypt, but how their own grandparents
left Lithuania for South Africa, how they had
to leave South Africa for England. Beside me,

Dannie from Belfast tells me about his mother:
how she danced in Theresienstadt. His wife,
Gretel, has stories of Dresden. We pause

to eat the bitter herbs, drink the first glass of wine.
Our host lifts the bottle, examines the label:
"This white is a Paarl wine, Laborie superior—

> Evening on the north slopes of Laborie, the sun
> setting away towards the Cape. Nkulu waits
> on the track for his father to come back from
> work. There are things he'd like to ask.

bought it on our last visit to the vineyards."
The explanations continue: we recite the ten
plagues, spill a drop of wine for each one.

Then the meal and songs of commemoration
and the promise, "Next year in Jerusalem."

> The sun is in Nkulu's eyes: his father, paid in kind
> reels towards his son, passes unseeing, and
> Nkulu knows that tonight, like last night and
> all other nights, there won't be anything to eat.

Winter Visit: Johannesburg in June

I'll not take home the chore of fire making,
the riddling of cinders, heavy tipping of ash,
collection of kindling with an underfoot snap.

I'll leave behind the screwing up of newspapers,
the oily smell of firelighters, sweeping the grate
into an obstinate dustpan, coaldust on my fingers.

I'll take with me the sudden gas-blue flame-burst,
the crackle and spark from creosoted wood,
and the long slow rise of flame after flame

their hot yellow petals sun-flowering the room;
then the late evening ember-glow with you knees-
up on the floor cushions, me on the distant sofa,

as we talk through the best of the day—a sunlit owl
roosting high in a palm; a fluffy bundle of puppy;
look forward to his friendly dogginess as he grows.

Sterkfontein Caves

(For Laila Josephine Nair Cashdan)

We took you to Sterkfontein slung low
on your dad's chest, your head under
his protecting hand. The guide did his best
patter-talk to get you on your first cave trip
but your dad turned around at the entrance,
the passage ways too low for baby-crawling.

So mother and grandmother, we make this journey
now without you, to our fossil ancestors down
under, to *Mrs Ples* lying where she fell into the dark,
queen of the night for over two million years,
perhaps a hunter-warrior like the Nairs of Kerala
who crossed the Indian Ocean a hundred years ago.

We kick our way through orange chert and breccia,
go down following the ancient water path along
the dolomitic rock wall with fossil fern décor,
into spiked caverns of electric-lit stalactites; stand
for a silent minute, recreate the blast of dynamite
that exploded the skull of *Mrs Ples* into history.

We look up into shafts of daylight overhung with
the green of white stinkwood, wild olive. Bent double
we edge along the homeward passages, climb the last
steps to where you are watching your dad drink his
heritage coke. We hear your cry for milk challenge
the wing-stretch screech of the hadedas overhead.

Pilanesberg

A volcanic alkaline ring complex extinct
for one thousand two hundred million years.
We drive in through the Kwa Maritane Gate
on the red dirt road paralleling the ring fence.
The car ahead of us turns into an elephant
glumly stalking a weeping wattle. We side
track it but it is uninterested in people.
Back on the red road we glimpse the herd
trunk to tail through the scrub, the baby
like the one in our car, cared for by adults.

Party pooper lightning flashes in the western sky
rain lashes the windscreen, we see nothing till
we drive out into the clear again, thunder
rolling away over Matlhorwe, the highest peak.
Now six warthog piglets scurry after their mum
zebra stripes mesmerise in a rump and flank glide,
giraffe keep their haughty high distance. We tick
wildebeest and white ringed toilet seat buck on
our species list. Midday the big cats won't play.
But a black backed jackal slides along a gully.

At Ratlhogo Waterhole the buffalo walk in
to drink, turn their heads like Lawrence's snake
Their horn ringed stare challenges our whispers
and then they are gone as quietly as they came.
The same silence at Mankwe Dam: heron stand
grey against blue water, springbok, zebra browse,
the only aggression the flap of the tiny long-
tailed widow bird chasing off the blue waxbill.
Just before leaving through Bakubung gate
the baboons sit in the grass, send us off.

The Lusiads 2005

We turn off the freeway to Orange Farm
one time Afrikaner farmlands, now scrub
and shackland-home to the jobless homeless;.
turn again for Thula Mtwana, our four-by-four
bumping the dirt track, orange dust swirling
in our wake. Halt at the square, queue waiting
for taxis, post office and bread shack,
a huge green water tank.

Two boys hoik their plastic water-carriers,
twice their own weight, on to a wheelbarrow,
smile for our camera. We drive on past
corrugated shacks, roofs held down
with stones; people stare because
they have nothing to do but stare.
Public portaloos stand Tardis-like
along the track, slow time-travelling
bringers of infection and disease.

Michael, broad-daylight pissed, tells us
ten years he's waited for a house, and
still he waits and dances before the camera:
"Shoot me, shoot me," he lisps through
broken teeth. We shake his shaking hand,
drive on to the human rights ceremony
at St. Lucia's church. Jose Barroso,
EU president from Portugal, comes bearing
gifts: blue baseball caps, promises of aid
in exchange for songs and smiles.

"There is always something new
out of Africa," he quotes from Pliny.
"And Europe has special ties with Africa."
There is always something new out of Europe,
out of Portugal, ever since Diaz and da Gama
rounded the Cape. Barroso gets pap and spinach
for lunch, then bows out of the township.

We stay long enough to share four biscuits
between six small boys; film their grandmother
in her cabbage patch washing the leaves,
give her 20 rand, drive back to our shady suburb.

Naming Day

(For Mishka Ann Nair Cashdan)

Seventeenth March, Libera's day
spring to life, dance and play.

Monday's child is fair of face
Ann is *Chen*, full of grace.

Mishka is a Russian bear
not much fur and not much hair.

Mishka comes from *Me Ca El?*
Who's like God? Who can tell?

In Hindi lore a gift of love,
love all round, below, above.

Nair, Kerala warrior faces the world,
a smile, a cry with both fists curled.

Cashdan, a chestnut, tall and strong,
a bringer of mercy through this song.

Cape Town Geese: Constantia

I'm wanting to write about South Africa
maybe something about Robben Island
or the District Six museum, but then
these sun-dappled geese come waddling...

Attracted by voices on the TV trailing
through the barred window
these white visitors are talking Goose—
Gans in Afrikaans—not quite a sinister
hissing, more a friendly in-line gaggle,
stepping less high than the S.S,
a flat-web wobble on sprung grass,
angled necks beaming an orange beak
and beady eye.

Now they make for the plastic bucket, dip
their heads, climb over the edge, take turns
to paddle until goose aggression explodes
into splatter of feathered water. Calm again,
they twist their necks to preen, whisper
their soft-carpeted wing-flap, tuck heads
under into nine cool splashes of snow
gathered in the sun, a stillness that is not
quite still. Then alert once more, heads
cocked on sentry duty, ready to save
a threatened homeland, their necks make
patterns, alternate S's like ancient lyres.

Suddenly something unseen moves them
and with a padded flap and honk they are
gone.

Anne Barnard's South Africa

(Anne Barnard was the wife of the Secretary to the first British Governor of Cape Colony and went out to Cape Town with him in 1797)

1. Cape Town

She arrives early May in thick fog, sees nothing,
hopes for wild rocks, something terrifying
but as the mist clears she sees Table Mountain

and a respectable town, clean and correct,
contradicting her imagination which has
invented skyscrapers two hundred years

too early. She likes the novelty, wishes
her sisters beside her. She takes the best
view she can with her pencil and portfolio,

then writes it all down in her journal: Caffres
Hottentots, Unicorns, Mountains, Camel Opards,
Ostriches, flowers wild and tame, but she is

joking. Really she will draw and describe
only what she sees with her own eyes, and tell
her sisters what she feels about it all.

That first day on land she watches the slaves
come back from the eight-mile trek with
their loaded poles, a bundle of firewood

at each end; and next day she sees the fat
Dutch women, their children and men,
each attended to Church by a slave

carrying an umbrella of green silk against
the African sun. Although it's Autumn
the flies are still as thick on the breakfast

pastries as the fleas in the mattress. For now
she must be a good wife and hostess in the Castle
till they find their own house called Paradise.

2. Visitors to Paradise

The name of the house already given
the Barnards take the place, make it home.

Sometimes hyenas poke their noses in
to pass verdict on Anne's hens.
One morning an old man-baboon comes
sauntering down from Table Mountain
looking for fruit. She has forbidden
whipping and shooting, but frightened,
her husband shoots, is electrified
by the creature's groan as it limps away.
He promises to spare them now and
in return she will help in the early morning
mosquito hunts. Today she watches
her visiting monkey: pays him with
bread to de-flea the dogs in the bits
they can't reach. An old slave charms
her as he plays, talks to his *marimba*.

Back home in England, my bird-visitors fly
overhead in swirls up to Hutcliffe Woods.
Squirrels perch on the shed roof, then run
behind the lilac. Mornings here are slug
trails shining on the doormat. Woodlice
move slowly, give up, lie with upturned hulls.
First caller is milk in four o'clock dark.
Then newspaper and lazy last the letters
scatter. Not quite like Paradise.

3. Looking for Anne Barnard in Swellendam

We're on our way from Plett to Cape Town
hurrying west because your girlfriend's
flying in from the States. I want to take it easy,
do the Garden Route like a proper tourist.

We slow down past Mossel Bay. This is
where Diaz came ashore and the Hottentots
showered him with stones. You tell me about
the gas works which sparkle in the dark

like something magic. Built as Apartheid's
answer to fuel sanctions, their lights will
be extinguished soon. Our country guest-
house seems like a bit of old England.

Next morning, we stop at Swellendam back
two hundred years to look for Anne Barnard.
We catch her on the stone outside the stables,
taking her picture of the *Drosty*, government

house, with two black girls digging by the door.
When we go inside she's at work on a portrait
of the *Landrost's* daughter, a romping girl
whom she'd love to have as her own child.

We don't see the bed with chocolate taffeta,
nor the French crayon beauties on the wall,
and no sign of the snakeskin given to her
by the *Landrost*. "Time to leave!" you say,

but I won't budge till I've seen the sashes
Anne gives to the womenfolk. I want to wave
her off with her husband, watch the *Landrost*
hoist the flag and the cannon fire a salute.

Cold beef would have been a more useful send-off,
she says, but perhaps less glory for King George.
We laugh at Anne Barnard's cynical humour.
I wonder what she would make of your impatience.

4. Anne Barnard Wears Her Husband's Trousers

Anne tells her niece it's like St. Peter's
among churches, like the King of Prussia
among generals, like Pitt among statesmen,
but the girl won't join the expedition—
there are no ballrooms on Table Mountain.
So they wave her goodbye, six o'clock

in the early cool of a summer morning.
They're on horseback and the slaves
carrying the baggage: food, tables, tents,
trowels for digging, bags for collecting.
The path winds through rocks and trees,
yellow waboom and pink suikerbossie.

Her husband laughs at her attire.
"First time you've ever been conscious
of my wearing them," she calls to him.
Then she dismounts, too steep for horses.
Mentor, one of her slaves, helps her up
the perpendicular slope of moving stones

studded with bits of leather where the mountain
has made old shoes of new. They stop for
port wine in a hillside cave, where escaped
slaves have left their marks, empty now.
Anne is away up the next thousand feet, ahead
of everyone. "Brave Vrouw," says Mentor.

At the top she looks down on a miniature world,
feels unembodied, as if she's floating free.
She paddles the thin pools, digs for bulbs,
collects white pebbles. "Gentlemen," she calls
across the top of the world, "God save the King!"
Their voices send King George echoing round

the Lion's Head, the Lion's Rump, the Hottentots,
till his name dies away in the distant valleys.
She sets up her painting table, takes the sun
setting beyond Robben Island in the far Atlantic.
The slaves prepare supper. They pitch the tents
and she's curled next to her husband all night.

Next day on the way down she takes more sketches,
Cape Town from above, no-one's done it before.
Back at the house she hangs her paintings, lays out
the pebbles, plants her bulbs, relives each moment;
consoles her niece for missing out on the memories.
But Anne's niece is dreaming of her next ball gown.

Macbeth

Last week you rang from Johannesburg.
wanted a recipe for cinnamon cake.
"Put the two mixtures in anyhow," I said,

"they always run together as it cooks."
Tonight you ring again from the theatre—
it's Macbeth in Zulu and you don't know the plot.

I remember the fifteen-year-olds struggling
with Shakespeare. Then it was Macbeth,
Scotland's striker, wanting to be manager,

bumped off Duncan, ran the team himself,
couldn't keep his best players, sacked
Banquo; Macduff resigned, joined England.

Neither Macbeth nor his wife could get
a proper night's sleep after that. His wife
died and Macbeth found he'd scored

nothing but own goals, the last one thinking
he was a match for Macduff. Macbeth lost
Scotland and his head. Duncan's son took over.

"Well, there's this fellow Buthelezi, O.K.?
ambitious sort of bloke, envies Mandela,"
I say, desperate to squash a five-act play

and the whole of South Africa into a long-
distance telephone call. "Got the picture,"
you say, "cheers, it's about to start."

Threads from *The Same Country*

The Smell of Poetry

Today it seems the post is full of poetry,
glossy brochures for readings, workshops,
festivals, and the competition industry.

A letter from Californ ia: my cousin Lily has read
Szymborska's poems, compared the Polish
with the English. The only poem not translated

tells how wagons with "sealed names" rode
at night across Poland, how the poet listened
for the wheels, (Lily heard them too) heard

"*tak toe*, *tak*, *tak toe*, *tak*." So it is, so it is.
And now the ring of that missing poem has
filled my living room with other absences.

Next in the pile, this packet won't open,
I have to use a knife to wrench the staples
and then I'm sliding into half-known Russian,

the poems of Gennady Aygi, into his rustlings,
ever deeper into the snows of Chuvash country.
I do my best in his Cyrillic whisperings.

Aygi takes me to Budapest, forces my hand
into the bronze hand of Raoul Wallenberg,
his words come down and startle where I stand.

I pick up the last envelope. Its red-rope logo
SENSE, a packet of pot-pourri, please help
the deaf-blind. My hands smell: *tak*, *tak toe*.

Red

(based on a textile hanging by Michika Oka)

I am looking for the story in your red tangle of threads:
your mother and how she helped to knot and splice
the fishing nets, pulled them wide over the harbour wall.
I hear her voice as she waits for her lover, calling across
the sun-rinsed water, safely calling his boat back.

Now she is deep embroidering her wedding dress, poppies
sewn on to red silk, and the threads shake out their flames.
And when they lie together the first night she will see
the sign in the bed, will scrub her knuckles raw washing
out the stain and will rejoice in the obstinacy of blood.

Then more long months of waiting for the boat until one day
when the autumn trees are set alight, he will come, salt lips,
hands coloured iron-rust, fish scales silvering his shirt.
And she will be straining for the baby's head to enter,
will know the slipstream of its body beyond her thighs.

A glimpse of red-beaked tern diving into the wake and
he's ashore tying the painter, the boat drawn alongside,
and there's the child's cry in the blood-curtained room,
and the midwife is soothing and stitching her torn flesh,
their parted lives woven into your matted shreds.

Elgar's D-O-G

(At the top of the pages of the manuscript of The Dream of
Gerontius, *Elgar wrote the word DOG for Dream of Gerontius. On
one page, however he wrote DAN, the name of his friend the
organist's bulldog.)*

Dream of Gerontius, the soul searching for peace-
but when the demons start up, they are snarling dogs.
As a child no dogs, only madmen from the asylum
yapping behind walls as I walked home from school.

Dogs have always splashed through my music—
polkas and quadrilles for the Lunatic Asylum band,
calming episodes for unquiet minds. The eleventh
Enigma is Dan, George Sinclair's bulldog.

We walk the banks of the Wye, George thinks organs,
I am planning something orchestral. Dan is dreaming
riverbank mud, the smell of decaying bulrushes, when
splash, Dan's in the river, tumbled head-over-paws.

Dan rights himself, struggles upstream, paddling
to keep up with our laughter. He leaps to the bank,
barking at the moorhens, shaking the water off
his wet coat: "Set that to music," says George.

At the recording studios, they show me pictures:
the gramophone on the table, the huge horn,
and the little dog listening to His Master's Voice.
Dan and his master are dead now, but he's caught,

caught in notes, in cadences, not only his mad upstream
swim in *Enigma*, but his dogginess is hidden too in
The Dream of Gerontius, and in my symphonies.
How curiously music has to carry its burdens.

Today, I have been out with Mina, my cairn terrier;
she wears her goggles, her veil, her pearls, she's a
little Duchess. My spaniel Marco leads her a dance.
My last composition, perhaps Mina dreaming Dan.

Playing Fields

October 1944, a dark corridor, our sixth form
history group crouched over seventeenth century
Europe: subject, causes of the Thirty Years War.

We imagine the castle in Prague, heated arguments
between Protestants and Catholics, and then—
strangely—the defenestration. No windows

in this corridor, only the bricked up spaces
where the air raid shelters have blacked out
the light. Elizabeth, the Winter Queen, reigns

briefly till the Battle of the White Mountain
sends her into exile and the war's in full swing.
At break we play hockey on a muddy field,

muscle up for the County Trials. History can wait.
Today the sun slants through the castle windows,
and here I am in Prague, peering into the ditch

updating the defenestration with photos and notes.
Later in the Pinkas Synagogue I stare at a picture
by Anita Spitzova, drawn on brown paper in Terezin:

six girls dance in a green field, they hold hands,
a pale sun sheds no light. The catalogue details
Anita's life: born 1933, brought to Terezin 1942,

deportation to Auschwitz October 1944.

One Way or Another

1. The Right Vocabulary

She has to find a way, doesn't matter
which way. There are worm-tracks in
the stone, soft bodies like snippets of

wool, cut from the edges of something
knitted a long time ago, its history lost:
something her mother crocheted—or

the sewing threads frayed away from
something bigger which the older woman
abhorred patterning the swept carpet.

There are no colours—just the raised
pathways leading her on till they die
out, leave her without directions.

2. Learning the Craft

She knows that proper sewing starts
with pinning on the pattern, but the
way-upness defeats her. She strains
for something she can recognise:

the upthrow and downthrow where
the rocks have haded after the fault.
That's a word she knows. It belongs
to her, they pinned it on her long ago.

Now the lines are traced, she follows
the curls through every tangle, thinks
she may be getting somewhere, if only
she had the patience for needlework.

3. Embroidery

Every summer holiday she'd labour
at a tray-cloth, ready for her mother's
end of August birthday. Lazy-daisy
leaf-border, purple herringbone flowers.

The linen surface would pull and tug
at the threads like a moving thing
that flowed with its own life, had
no regard for her struggling fingers.

Sedentary afternoons filled with
knotted cottons, blunt needles.
Neither mother nor child could sew:
the traycloths were seldom used.

4. Sedimentary

The spaces between rocks fill
with the green leaf of mallow,
the polished slickenside of rock
no longer calcite-limestone, more

malachite. She turns from surfaces
to deeper things, to things dug up,
fossils buried by seatides millions
of years ago. There are messages

in the rocks, graptolite signs encoded
by plant-animals waiting now to be
deciphered. She remembers picking
them idly from gravel paths where

her children went to school, has sung
their choral tunes on the church altar,
its grey stone quarried in distant hills
carrying the curls and frills of ammonite.

This summer she's seen them again
held in the polished limestone steps
she climbed to her daughter's house,
core of belemnite, scarab trilobite.

5. Story-telling

The drawers stuffed with crumpled
embroidery, the shelves of stone,
skull ands fossil, the odd shapes

of dead-wood birds and snakes,
found in wet fields, on river banks
and salty shorelines; their signals

from other times ignite old loves
and hates she'd thought forgotten.
Wind blows over the stump-work

of these images quilted the colours
of water avens, early purple orchids,
forget-me-nots, the shaped candles

of lords-and-ladies, sea-lily crinoids.
Light has faded to murk but now
the reef-knolls have been explored,

the faunal markerbands stitched up,
she can start on the drawn-thread-
work through the troubled calcite.

The Same Country

1. History Re-enacted: Creswell Crags, July 2000

A cold day for heritage but here we come
along the river, marvelling at the crags,
pocked limestone, the tree cover; adjust
our helmets ready for exploration: the guide
puts on her Victorian Ella Boyd Dawkins smile,

with black skirt, Doc Martens, straw hat.
"My father," she says, "is a wonderful man.
Picked and shovelled through ten thousand years,
a hundred thousand years, back to an ice age."
She takes up the huge shin bone, challenges us

to guess at the mammoth, the hyena teeth-
marks. An older woman in anorak says:
"What's a nice Victorian young lady
like you doing here?" The girl smiles,
is not fazed: she carries on with her guide-

book patter, learnt so carefully, shows us
the bone charm round her neck. "My father
will take this for the museum, it's not mine."
We laugh till the years run into each other.

2. The Child is Father of the Man: William Boyd Dawkins, 1845

Dark down here with a black smell
and I'm not sure I like it.
Punishment, my father says,
because I interrupted him.

There's a glint of light from the grating.
I know where it is on the pavement,
a circle of black ironwork flowers
and when the coalman comes
he lifts it up, shucks the bag
and a stream of shining pieces
goes chuckling into the depths,
as if they're going back down
to where they came from.

Now as I wait a million years for them
to let me back up, I listen for their footsteps,
hear my father's voice saying prayers
for my obedience. In my hand a small lump of coal.
In the tiny ray of light it seems like something
comes alive on the surface, a leaf from the old forests,
real millions of years ago. My secret find.

3. William Boyd Dawkins finds the Horse's Head, 1876

Carved on this piece of broken rib hidden
in the top layers of Robin Hood's Cave.
Twelve thousand years old. I found it.

Think on the man who cut into the bone,
worked with his flint knife, made these
incisions, brown lines on the white base;

outlined the thick-set head, the wide neck,
flared nostril, unblinkered eye. Think how
he knew to show the wind in the mane

blowing forward against the jet-stream,
and the lines across the horse, a flicker-
fence he gallops through, some ancient

Ascot to speed him into the carver's
winning dreams. And into my hands.
Quietly at home with resin and paint

my wife helps to remake the bone, re-carve
the horse. Now in his glass case, he runs non-
stop, carrying us back into the last Ice Age.

4. The Revd. Magens Mello has his say, 1877

Robin Hood's Cave, no outlaws
but a quiet place for reverence,
I come here often with my painting stool,
watercolours and paper to paint
the green lushness softening the crags,
where soon the wonders of God's Creation
will explode upon the minds of men.

Today we have come with picks, shovels,
colliers from Creswell, hired labourers
from the Welbeck estate, myself and
archaeologists, Boyd Dawkins and Heath,
to search the layers of the past.

It is God's work we do, just as Sundays
at Brampton Church I search God's words
to find how we are meant to live in love
and grace. It is all one grand design.
Or should have been till Tom the collier
comes across the tooth: great find this tooth
from the Lesser Scimitar Cat. Dawkins'
face is lit with inner light of revelation.

Back at the Rectory, comfortable with
after-dinner port, Heath voices doubts,
says the time-scale's wrong, the cat
has been extinct three hundred thousand
years, this layer's not that old. He smiles,
ready to make his attack: "Maybe Dawkins
placed it there himself! You know, a bid
for fame, before he's really worth it."

I take a sip of port, knowing the ways of men
to be more devious than the ways of God.
"Some of these early hunters," I say,
"they weren't out to make it easy for us.
This tooth, now, maybe was a hunter's charm
found years before he came to the Crags;
wore it as an ornament round his neck.
Imagine him going home, the wife all smiles
till she sees what he has lost."

"The trouble with you men of the cloth,"
says Heath, "you're always so rational."
There are many things to thank God for.

5. Creswell and Buxton Souvenirs, July 2000

Mostly the kids want ice-cream
but ice-cream melts,
leaves only a sticky trace that washes out.
I'd like them to go for something longer-lasting:
a booklet or a crafted model.

On the way home I drive into Creswell village
ready for re-discovery, catch voices of the pupils
I once taught, trapped behind boarded school windows;
look for the pithead wheel silent since the strike;
imagine the darkness below crumbling
the coal-cutter, rotting the unmoving belts;
the acrid smell bottled for good.

Two youngsters on the street corner
kick at the grass emerging between
the paving stones.

Later in the Buxton museum I stare into
Boyd Dawkins' study, a reconstructed space
covered in a layer of brown Victorian gloom.
Tables littered with his collections: books
and bones, rocks, vases, paintings and masks.

I lean on the glass-case barriers, work out
each item named in the key: bits and pieces
waiting to be put together. No sign of Ella.

From *Laughing All the Way*

The Tyre-Cairo Letters

(Expanded from a fragment of parchment in the John Rylands Library, Manchester.)

1. Sadaka to his father: Tyre, October 1090

Father, they've given the post of cantor
to someone else—
do you remember the blue day of hope
I left Cairo with the oarsmen singing?
—to a pimply youth who intones without feeling
and an abominable accent.
Today is the first of Ramadan and the town
is on edge. The Jews keep close.
The streets are wet with the first
of the winter rains.
Give me your blessing. I am married now.
(You hoped Bathsheva Bat Eliahu
would be your new daughter.)
But give me your blessing even so.
lt is Elisheva Bat Shmuel who has
found favour in my eyes.
Now the name of Sadaka Ha Levi will
sound here in Tyre over the generations
when our sons and our sons' sons
are called in the synagogue.
I am in good health. I sing every day.
I send a son's love to my mother.
Sadaka Ha-Levi Ben Solomon.

2. Bathsheva to Sadaka Ha Levi: Cairo, October 1090

Cairo is hot and I long for you.
Since you left I have done nothing
but weaving every day till my back aches,

my finger joints stiffen.
Today, my little brother pulled the threads
now they lie tangled on the floor tiles
making new patterns where the old are worn
I cannot sort out the wools:
Mother has cut the knotted lumps out
like some hideous growth
but the frayed ends hang forlorn.
She will beat Isaac for what he has done
but Father will praise him because he learns so well.
He will not see the red and blue bruises on Isaac's back.
Now I am sad.
I want my weaving ready for your return
but I do not know how to finish it.

3. The matchmaker to Sadaka's father: Cairo, December 1090

Honourable master, it is seven months now
since you visited me with your son.
I found him an excellent match
a young girl well-provided for.
Her father's storehouse has silks and woollens,
you could not do better.
She is comely into the bargain:
her skin the colour of olives
her teeth white as a sheep's fleece
her eyes blue as the blown glass of Tyre.
Why has your son gone to that far off city
where the young girls are lewd and ugly?
The marriage has been arranged
and you must pay me the ten gold coins.
I am old now, I have waited too long:
my house needs a roof
before the winter rains destroy me.

4. Aviva Bat Solomon to her brother Sadaka: Cairo, December 1090

Distant brother, you say you are married now.
How I wish you could unsay those words.
Father has received your letter
but he will not reply.
His wrath is the wrath of a jealous God:
the women of the family keep silent
while his anger roars through the house,
a hot wind in the season of the chamsin.
He walks the streets alone, his head to one side
unable to face Bathsheva's menfolk.
Your news is whispered from hearth to hearth
and the bales of wool that should have come
as Bathsheva's dowry gathers dust in her father's shop.
Mother fears for Father's business
dreads that hunger will be the guest at our table.
I have no blessings to send you
only the wailings of a sad sister
who curses the white boat and those singing
oarsmen who rowed you to Tyre.

5. Elisheva Bat Shmuel to her mother-in-law: Tyre, January 1091

Strange Mother, whom I have never met
I send you greeting from Tyre.
Now that I am one with your son
I shall love you as a dutiful daughter.
As the new moon pulls the tides of the sea
so each month my body will be prepared
and when my hopes are washed away
in that unclean flux
I shall be cleansed in the Mikvah
and my womb will be dedicated
to the grandchildren you desire.

Greet Ya'acov, the little brother whom I do not know
and kiss Aviva, my new sister
whom I long to meet.
How I envy the white birds who fly
to strange lands and new homes.
Though I cannot fly, my heart has wings.

6. Solomon to his son Sadaka: Cairo, April 1091

Since you left, my fortunes have run dry
and I long for your return.
Today we have had the ceremony to mark
the rising of the Nile.
Kettledrums have sounded these three days,
trumpets have blasted our ears.
The stones of Cairo echo the hoofbeat
and march of the Caliph's army.
Men of wisdom have ridden with the princes
and your Uncle with the doctors of the court.
The Caliph dismounts at the head of the canal,
hurls his spade to make the first breach
and the slaves attack with pick and shovel:
the Nile floods.
The waters are blessed by the giving of alms
to the deaf-mutes in the first boat.
Now the markets of the city will swell
with the fruits of the earth,
but in my hearth there is an emptiness.

7. Bathsheva to Sadaka: Cairo, July 1091

So you are married. I wish you well.
Now I am without the ties which held
me to you, I am a new person.
The days of weaving are gone, the lengths
of cloth which might have been my dowry
are sold and I am glad. Some other
woman can enjoy those coloured threads

which bound me for so many months.
I have opened a school. Women from Fustat
leave their blind teachers, come to our house.
I have collected flowers and herbs
and your uncle has named them for me.
Today I used tincture of iodine for a cut hand,
kaolin for a stomach that cannot keep its food.
I have begun to study the occulist's art.
Soon I shall see into the ways of men.

8. Sadaka to his father: Tyre, April 1096

There is bad news from Constantinople:
they say the Franks are moving east.
Travellers speak of massacres in Blois
a thousand Jews killed in Mainz.
The Franks want Jerusalem for their
three-in-one god and I fear for our safety.
The Caliph has increased our taxes
to pay for the defence of Tyre.
The town is full of snorting horses
and the flash of Muslim scimitars.
If you are willing to receive us in your house
we shall leave this threatened town
sail the blue road back to Cairo.
The curse of war will be lifted from us,
you will greet your granddaughters
and their shining faces will bless your old age.

9. Sarah to her son Sadaka: Cairo, September 1096

My dearest son, your father is dead:
he died in the quiet of the night
in the new moon of Tishrei.
We have sat on low stools,
said Kaddish every day for seven days.
Now I must put aside my mourning:
there is work to be done.

Your sister Aviva has a good head for sums,
today she counted, sorted the bales.
I have employed three men from Fustat,
dyers who have brought their own vats,
installed them in the outside sheds.
The wood is rotten and I fear we shall have
dye leaking into the courtyard.
Worse still, Ya'acov spends his time
with these men when he should be learning.
There is no-one to tell him—if only your father—
but such thoughts are useless:
dyed cloth makes a good profit.

10. Elisheva Bat Shmuel to her sister-in-law: Tyre, December 1096

Sister, Aviva, I write to you
though we know each other only by name.
One woe follows on the heels of another.
Sadaka is dead.
The Franks fired the synagogue in Antioch:
he had gone there to sing Kaddish. The rabbis
tell us we should not grieve:
the dead have found a safe harbour
but his was too short a journey.
Now I shelter with the widow, Leah
but fear of the Franks is all around us.
I do not know how long Tyre will be safe.
Leah has ships bound for Cairo
with cargoes of tabby carpets
rose and violet-water in Tyre glass.
We will cross the sea that brought Sadaka here.
You will have a new sister to help
with the dyestuffs and your mother a new daughter.
As women we shall be strong, give each other comfort
and my daughters will grow in a place of peace.

Sisters and Others

Just Realised I'm In This Photo—

I see them standing there outside Trinity College
Jack in his mortar board, gown, and scowl;
Mother in her cloche hat, Father in his bowler.
They've driven up to Cambridge in the Buick
for Jack's graduation. Mother is pregnant,
bump not visible yet under her black swing coat.
Father is doing well, the General Strike is over,
and the wool business is paying dividends,
the slump still keeping its end up, World War II
hasn't happened yet, not even Franco in Spain.

I want to tell them about Jack—it's that
he's not interested in business, in wool,
not even in science, though his degree
is in physics. He likes languages, likes
language. I want to shout: "Don't push
him, he'll hate the business, let it go to ruin."
But you can't be heard from the womb.

Birth Day

It was a foggy November morning, yellow light
filtering through net curtains into the bedroom.
My exit and entrance was filled with a cry
I didn't know belonged to me.

Then they all came and looked, peered round
the pale purple curtains pulled back on the cradle.
Jack came first but those twenty-one years were
too big a gap: he could have been my father.

Ruth came last, only just tall enough to peep over
the side, and there were smiles which meant love
but also *you're my little sister, don't mess with me,*
you'll never quite catch up my five year start.

Other faces came and went. There were rich smells
and whisperings and touchings. And my own fingers
which I hardly knew I had, clenched, unclenched,
and found their way to my inquisitive mouth.

My last memory of that first hour of life is the taste
of milk, and the tinkling of the piano downstairs
where Jack was playing duets all on his own,
and I wiggled my unknown toes and burped a smile.

Toffee

We'd come to see Father Christmas in his grotto
but his moustache drooped into his smile.
I couldn't look at him: "I do want a present
but he's ugly and I won't shake his hand."
My mother said nothing, just pulled my sleeve
and we went down to the food hall.

The toffees were piled up on display tables
covered in crinkly red paper.
The gold wrappers shone in the shop lights.
I wanted a toffee—I didn't need one
but I needed to steal one.
Mother was talking to Mrs Neroslavsky.
Her red hat bobbed across my mother's face.
I put out my right hand, took a toffee, clenched
my fist around it, imagined the caramel taste,
how I would smooth out the twisted ends
of the gold wrapper on the kitchen table.

Going up in the lift from the basement
they went on talking hats and gloves.
We went out into December sunlit frost,
stood by the orange warning flashes
of the Belisha Beacon, waited
for the traffic and the gossip to stop.
"Say goodbye to Mrs Neroslavsky."
I said "Goodbye Mrs Neroslavsky,"
held out my left hand. "No, your right,"
said my mother. I held out the toffee.
It burned bright on my tilted palm.

Mother's hand swept across mine
and the gold butterfly-toffee flew
up into the air, then dropped into
the gutter. "How dare you!"
She held my hand all the way home
my blue wool gripped in her red leather.

Older Sister

You gave me Oliver Twist but I couldn't read it
well not till years afterwards. You took me to see
Puss in Boots but I didn't understand the rules
of pantomime, and I wished it was all over.
I think it was a treat to make up for the dentist,

Mr Shkolnikoff's with those disgusting orange
leather seats in the waiting room: their smell
made me sick even before we got upstairs and
I climbed into that awful chair and the great big
drill which made enough noise and vibration

to dig through to Australia got into my mouth
and I bit Mr Shkolnikoff's finger so he put
a metal ring on to protect himself which meant
there was even more cold metal in my mouth
just added to the taste of cloves and amalgam.

And then downstairs by the glass cabinet you pointed
to the green and yellow tubes of Kolynos toothpaste
and I knew of course that he had made the stuff
it's name a sort of anagram of his own, not that
I could read it, or his for that matter—just the sound

of Shkolnikoff and Kolynos made me know that teeth
and being Russian were somehow a family secret and
when I got the blue china bunny-rabbit for a present
it was you who told me that the hole where the cotton
wool came out was the way babies were born,

and I said, "Don't be silly," but then the next day
I got up early in the cold of winter, slid across the lino
into your bedroom, wanting to climb into your bed,
and I stopped short to see you lying there uncovered,
a great white sanitary towel between your legs.

Reading on the Loo

Somehow I got the idea it was wicked
so I promised God each time I wouldn't do it again
well, not if he kept his part of the bargain
and arranged for Mother to take me swimming.

But she thought swimming baths were dirty,
and libraries—so I couldn't borrow books. My books
came from Foyles Children's Book Club:
Susannah of the Mounties, *Swallows and Amazons*,

and the *Twins*, *Spartan*, *Persian* and *Dutch*.
My mother wasn't as bad as my grandmother
who kissed her prayer book when it fell on the floor.
Our lavatory had brown stucco walls, dark lino—

a place of sin without further sinning so
I sat there waiting for the Syrup of Figs
to do its worst without the help of a book.
Sycamore leaves rattled the window, smells

of cabbage drifted up from the kitchen below.
Sometimes, I broke my side of the bargain,
and rode away to *The Far-Distant Oxus* across
Exmoor to Peran Wisa with Anthony and Frances,

or sailed across Windermere with Titty and John:
their mother didn't seem to mind about dirt.
The books were pink-cloth bound, the paper thick,
and I couldn't always keep my promise.

Bagatelle

The box stood tall as me on the bus home.
We carried it up Netherhall Gardens, laid it out
on the nursery table. "Big girls first," you said
as usual, and pulled the trigger. One after
the other the silver balls shot round the board,
our wows and eyes rolling in unison:
one hundred and fifty every ball.

I pulled the trigger, a ball jerked up a few inches,
slid back into the starting block. I tried again,
gave it all I'd got: the ball whizzed round, hit
the bouncing pin, a moment's hesitation—
and it dribbled pitifully to the bottom of the board.
No score.

It's like that with the piano. Beethoven's
Bagatelle in E flat: your fingers bounce from
B flat, to G, to E flat, your big-girl hands
take off, flying up and down the keyboard.
My left hand struggles through arpeggios,
right hand appoggiatura a glottal stop—
then runs dry into a rickety trickle.
No sound.

Afraid

of waves. Always have been since the day
you pulled me into the sea on a Norfolk beach,
out of my depth, a big sister keen to show
her little sister how not to be afraid.
And we were both tumbled over and over,
spluttering for breath, flailing for foothold.

Mother stood on the dry sand not knowing
whether to be cross with your daring or
thankful that we were both walking towards
her. Crossness always won out with her.
So now whenever I'm overcome in the break
of waves, I hear Mother's scolding voice,
sometimes even feel the slap of her hand.

Anorak

(For Ruth: 1923–2009)

When I saw the blue anorak on your door last year
I teased: "Don't be surprised if I whip that off the hook
when I leave, mine's worn out, yours still good as new."

We'd bought them together on one of your visits
bargain-hunting in York, then walked, two sisters
in green and blue along Froggatt Edge, along
the Derwent path beside the reservoir, saw the larches
spring froth, the white fall of foam over the dam.
Then you went back to Israel to a closed-in room.

I went on walking until the cuffs on my anorak frayed
and the zips fell apart. Today I stand in your empty room
want to tell you I'm taking your anorak back to England—

next week I'll be wearing it somewhere on the hills.

You're Gone Now—

too late for me to tell you I'm writing this.
But last year we talked poetry
and you wrote a brilliant poem
about imaginary people in our childhood garden.

Before that you were a doctor
who made children better
and tracked them year by year.

Before that you shared a skeleton
with Mercy Bing who married Norman Heatley
who helped discover penicillin.
And you wrote a poem about the skeleton.
Mercy still remembers you
though you're not here to remember her.

Earlier still we played together in the garden
and you told me stories about people you'd made up
and you made up magic potions that would make me better
if I'd scraped my knee when I fell down the steps
talking to the imaginary people like Mrs Lemmar
who always admired our imaginary new hats.

Today when my leg swelled up
I had to imagine you.

Anna Playing the Flute

She frowns at the sheet music on the stand,
turns away because those black notes are worse
                              than words in a book: they jump
                    where they are not supposed
                                        to jump.

In her head the notes belong to each other, are held together
by rhythm and melody and her fingers hear what they have to do.

Her lips pursed, she blows and her body moves into the shape
of the arpeggio, into the octave leap
                              and off again
diving into Bach's *Anna Magdalena* as easily
                                        as she dives
              into water, with the same assuredness
              the same serenity she has when she swims.

The Airing Cupboard

At the bottom of a pile of old pillowcases
worn and torn through generations of use
I find a piece of white linen, drawn-thread work,
too small for a tablecloth, perhaps for a cot.

Who stitched this on long summer evenings
in a Finnish house by the sea, sitting on the veranda
two small boys and a golden-haired girl listening
to a story of Baba Yaga, the ugly witch who lived
in a house on stilts just like their Turku summer house,
the mother waiting for the fourth child who next year
will be carried to England in a bent willow hat box,

away from revolution, the clash of red and white armies.
and the golden-haired girl will forget she was once *Kuliki*
or *Zalotinkaya*, and she and her little sister will become
proper English children in tunics and straw panamas.

The Garden

Things are happening here in the garden
where the bougainvillea winks in the sun
but I don't quite know what is happening.

Over there the dogs are running round the pool
barking at the sound of their own barking.
Here on this side of the fence, the girls

are climbing the rope ladder, sliding the slide
shouting at the sound of their own shouting.
And I am watching the man with the sun in his eyes.

They are his girls, and his dogs and he is my son
and he is calling them, the dogs and the girls,
"Chloe, Max, Laila, Mishka, Laila, Max, Chloe."

But the dogs go on running and barking,
and the girls go on shouting and climbing
and I go on watching him watching.

Afraid of Flying

1. Afraid

of flying, but I braved it that February half term,
flew to friends in Germany, you went to Cornwall.
I spent all week in a tourist blur thinking only
of how I'd get back home, vowed that was the last flight
I'd ever take till a few days later, we saw in the paper,

The Herald of Free Enterprise on its side, just clear
of Zeebrugge, doors wide open to the sea's inward rush,
boatswain and first officer each sure the other one
had closed the doors. That was the moment you chose
to tell me you'd be leaving to find your own space,
somewhere you could touch all four walls.

I've done a lot of solo flying since then.

2. Afraid

you were going to leave me? Never thought about it.
We had a delicate balance, flitted in and out of closeness,
gave each other wing space to flap and dart away.

So day after day once you had taken your things and gone,
I stood at the door like the River-Merchant's wife
waiting for her lord, the rice pot gently bubbling,

and I watched the paired butterflies in the buddleia
till I could tease myself no longer, turned into the house,
called up the hollow stairs, "Shall I put the kettle on, love?"

An Email for Every Occasion

Hi there Elisabeth/Lizzie/Liz

I am so sorry/glad to hear of Ruth's/Rachel's death/wedding.
I wish you/them long life.
Your granddaughter/nephew must be so thrilled/responsible
    to be a bridesmaid/executor.
I am sad/pleased to learn that you have had to retire/are still
    working.
I am sure that/uncertain if that will impinge
    positively/negatively on your health.
How awesome/awful that you are a published poet/a great-
    great aunt.
It's really well dark/cool about the rhododendron/the lilac
    being cut down/flowering so early.

It is a shame/lucky we are all so far away from/near each other.
All my condolences/congratulations
your cousin/daughter/sister/son

Lorna/Sarah/Ellen/Ben

Email to My Sister

(For Esther: born 1918 Finland, died 2011 Herzliya)

Hi there, I'm at my laptop with gmail open ready.
I've got the missing line of the Russian nursery rhyme
you couldn't remember last week, the one about
the old man who killed his dog, собаку, accusative.

Though you never did like thinking about the grammar,
just waited for the words and their endings to percolate
through from your childhood, your ear attuned so early
you cringed at my ugly English accent.

I've got the story finished about our brother, the one
where his widow gets rung up by an unknown son
she didn't know he'd had. And, oh, I'm just loving
those little biscuits, oreilles de cochons.

I'm halfway through typing up your notes about
your visit to the Durham coalfield after the strike.
They've published my article on real-life storytelling,
though I know you didn't like re-living the holocaust.

You spent your life getting people to move on, come
together. I've not yet tried your recipe for noodle pie,
and I forgot to ask you for the fruit cake one with
cherries and nuts and a faint taste of coffee.

Love. I'm going to press send now.

I Want It Now

Liz, you should have seen all the people,
how they came chatting and giggling,
old enemies admitting their faults,
youngsters who'd never really known you,
but said ok, they'd read a poem if they had to.
Even your ex-husband said a few ungrudging words.
You'd have loved it.

Thank you, but I want my funeral before I die.
I want to hear now, how kids love me as a writer,
how colleagues respected me, how I make
the best risen Yorkshire pudding, the sourest
blackcurrant kissel with just a hint of sweetness;
how my latest poems are about to be published;

how I looked after my mother for years;
how my sisters love their little sister,
how my own kids think I'm right-on,
laugh at me and let me laugh at them,
how their kids know I'm not bovvered,
so they don't like have to be bovvered either;

but I guess it's not cool to be at your own funeral—
whatever.

Bicycles

When the last dark bicycle day comes
I shall pedal uphill on Jacob's Ladder
to that great place in the sky where
every wheel will be winged
and I'll float through and beyond clouds
into the spaces and spheres from where
I'll look down to see my granddaughters
on their fairy bikes, pink and glossy
with furry saddles, pedalling madly
across the floor to move themselves
forward foot by tiny foot.

And when that fades and the wings
of my bicycle fold, I'll head down
the dark tunnel of that world without me
to a place where broken bikes clank
their chains, ring their unremitting
bells, and where maybe I can unlearn
the piston movement of knee and calf,
the balance between falling one way
or the other.

Acknowledgements

Some of these poems are taken from previous collections: *Laughing All the Way* (Five Leaves, 1995), *The Same Country* (Five Leaves, 2009).

Some of these poems were commended in competitions or appeared in journals/anthologies: Ver Poets, Ware Poets, Virginia Warbey Prize, Poetry Business Sheffield Prize, Basil Bunting Prize, Bridport Prize, McLellan Prize, *Scintilla*, *Stripe* (Templar), *Snap* (Templar), *Dancing with Delsie* (Leaf), *Versions of the North* (Five Leaves).